Tonga Toutai Pāletu'a
Faith and Testimony from the Pacific

Tonga Toutai Pāletu'a
Faith and Testimony from the Pacific

Siope Lee Kinikini
Tangiteina Pāletu'a Kinikini
'Akesiu Pāletu'a Vainuku

2019

© 2019 Siope Lee Kinikini

Tonga Toutai Paletu'a: Faith and Testimony from the Pacific

All rights reserved. No part of this publication may be reproduced, stored in a retrieval system or transmited in any form or by any means, electronic, mechanical, photocopying, recording or otherwise without the prior permision of the publisher or in accordance with the provisions of the Copyright, Designs and Patents Act 1988 or under the terms of any licence permitting limited copying issued by the Copyright Licensing Angency.

Published by: Siope Lee Kinikini

Cover and Text Design by: Siope Lee Kinikini

A CIP record for this book is acailable from the Library of Congress Cataloging-in-Publication Data

ISBN-13: 978-1-7332646-0-0

Distributed by: Siope Kinikini

For information about this book: skinikini@gmail.com

Printed and bound in the United States of America

Pāletu'a, n., shield, *fig.*, person to whom we habitually depend, protector.

Tongan-English Dictionary, Government of Tonga, 1955, p. 400.

Tonga Toutai Pāletu'a

Table of Contents

Foreword	vii
Preface	ix
Acknowledgments	xix
Chronology of events	xvi
Genealogy	xxv

Chapter 1 — 1

    Beginnings | 1923 - 1939

A New World	1
The Pāletu'a Family	1
Viliami and Milika Mafi Pāletu'a	2
Early Life	2
Apostasy in Tonga	5
Teen Years	6
Leaving Home	7
Schoolmates and Church	8
Testimony	9

Chapter 2 — 10

    Conversion | 1940 - 1949

World War II	10
Return Home and Baptism	11
Education, Teacher Training and Work	15
Courtship and Marriage	17
From Makeke to Liahona College	19

Pictures 1923 - 1950 — 21

Chapter 3 — 25

    Forward With Faith | 1950-1959

War Ends, Tonga is Noticed and Church Growth	25
Family Life Begins	26

Classes Begin at Liahona College	26
Liahona College	27
Working and Serving	30
Leaving Government Work for Liahona College	30
President David O. McKay Visits Tonga	32
Scouting in Tonga	32
Honesty, At All Cost	34
Back to Family	35
New Zealand Temple to be Sealed	36

Chapter 4 — 37
    Preparing the Way | 1960 - 1969

Queen Sālote passes away	37
Liahona, Radio, and Miracles	38
Formation of the Hihifo District	40
Mission Presidency with President Groberg	41
How Can I Serve When My Family is Falling Apart?	41
A New Stake in Tonga	44
The Parable of the *Makafeke*	46
First Trip to Salt Lake City, Utah	46
Graduation and a First Grandchild	48
The Church Growth Continues	49
Seeking a Christlike Life	50
Family Changes	53

Pictures 1950 -1960 — 54

Chapter 5 — 63
    Missionary Work | 1970 - 1979

LDS Business College for 'Akesiu	63
The Need for More Stakes in Tonga	63
"Unusual" Leadership	64
Respect for the servants of the Lord	66
'Akesiu's Marriage	67

Separated and Connected	67
The Tonga Nuku'alofa Mission	68
Every Detail is Important	71
The Importance of the Book of Mormon	72
A Focus on Gathering Israel	74
Invitations to preach in other churches	74
Open House in Sopu	75
Stake in Vava'u	75
The Temple is our Goal	76
Ta'u oe Kau Leimana	77
1976 Area Conference	77
Tongan Missionaries to other Lands	79
Regional Representative for the Twelve Apostles	79

Chapter 6 81
The Temple | 1980 - 1989

A New Temple in Tonga	81
Clearing the Land	82
Groundbreaking	83
Calling as the Temple President	85
Actual Construction on the Temple	86
Hurricane Isaac	88
Building a Temple in Tonga is Hard Work	88
Welcome, Brother	89
Temple President Training in Salt Lake City	90
The Angel Moroni	91
Open House	93
Prisoners Shall Go Free	94
Dedication	96
Temple Work Begins Immediately	97
The Paletu'a Family Together	97
One Year Celebration	98

Pictures 1960 - 1980 99

Chapter 7 113
                Endure to the End | 1990 - 2002

  Missionary Training Center 113
  100 Years of the Church in Tonga 114
  Farewell Brother Ermel Morton 115
  Heavenly Father is in Charge 116
  Visits From Dear Friends 118
  Pioneers of the Pacific Celebration BYU-Hawaii ... 119
  Review of the translation of the Book of Mormon ... 120
  Final years 120

Chapter 8 121
                Epilogue

  Posterity 121
  Tongans Outside of Tonga 121
  Other Side of Heaven 2: The Fire of Faith ... 123
  Missionary Work Continues 125
  Tongan Mission Presidents 126

Pictures 1980 - 2002 128

Chapter Notes 139
  Chapter 1 | Beginnings 139
  Chapter 2 | Conversion 141
  Chapter 3 | Forward with Faith 143
  Chapter 4 | Preparing the Way 144
  Chapter 5 | Missionary Work 145
  Chapter 6 | The Tonga Temple 146
  Chapter 7 | Preparing the Way 147
  Chapter 8 | Epilogue 148

The Priesthood Line of Authority 150
Glossary of Tongan Words 151
References 153

Foreword

When I returned to Tonga as Mission President in July 1966 with my wife Jean and our five young daughters one of the first orders of business was to choose two counselors to serve with me in the mission presidency. I felt good about keeping Manase Nau as my first counselor but wasn't sure about who should be second counselor.

To my knowledge I had never met Tonga Toutai Pāletu'a, as on my first mission I served only on Niutoputapu and in Ha'apai and Tonga Toutai was on Tongatapu. I interviewed many brethren but when I met with Tonga (who was serving as District President in Hihifo) I knew immediately that he should be my other counselor. The certainty of that calling has never left me.

Tonga was an excellent counselor and worked particularly well with the missionaries. He also handled a lot of difficult situations with the branches and districts. I missed him greatly when he was later called into the stake presidency and then as stake president and Patriarch, etc. When it was time for a Tongan to be called as mission president, I was given the assignment as a Regional Representative, to help in that process. I again had heaven's undeniable assurance that Tonga Toutai Pāletu'a should be that mission president. President Spencer W. Kimball felt the same way when he extended the call to him.

That same spirit prevailed when Tonga was called by President Kimball as the first President of the Tonga Temple. Tonga was close to the Lord and always did a wonderful work wherever he was called to labor.

On one occasion I gave Tonga a rather difficult assignment and asked how he felt about it. He replied, "I know the Lord. I know He prompts His leaders in their calls. I am not afraid to accept any call from the Brethren because I know the Lord will help me accomplish the task, whatever it is."

That is the faith I knew and felt from Tonga Toutai Pāletu'a. He is one of the great leaders from Tonga as well as from this planet. I am sure he is carrying on that faithful work and leadership on the "other side." I hope his posterity, as well as all people might follow his magnificent example.

Elder John H. Groberg

Preface

In 2015 I returned to the Kingdom of Tonga with my wife and ten-year-old daughter to pick my mother up from missionary service at the Nuku'alofa Temple and to help my daughter connect with her Tongan heritage. Although we visited many of the tourist sites on Tongatapu, I was particularly interested in showing my daughter a modest, three-room bungalow style home shrouded by plants and banana trees. The small home was barely visible from the road.

My grandfather and I built this small home when I was a teenager. This small home held profound memories for me. I stood there in silence, a flood of emotions washed over me like the ocean tide. Feelings I had forgotten over the years returned. I could almost hear the echo of voices now gone. I could feel tears flowing from my eyes as I remembered my grandparents and the things I had learned when I stayed with them as a teen.

When I was fourteen years old, I excitedly returned to the Kingdom of Tonga for a summer. I would celebrate my fifteenth birthday in Tonga. I remember thinking it would be the best summer of my life. I had plans of sleeping in, running around the island, and making new friends. I wanted to eat until I couldn't move and sleep until I regretted it. I saw myself spending afternoons on a beach. In my mind, it was going to be an exciting adventure, but my plans never happened.

My grandfather, Tonga Toutai Pāletu'a, had already planned out my entire summer in exact detail before I arrived on the island. The plan was to build a home adjacent to his larger home. The purpose of this "other" home was to provide a resting place for people who traveled long distances to attend the Temple. It would be a place for them to rest. As soon as I arrived in the Kingdom of Tonga, I began to work.

The schedule he had put in place was exact. I would wake up early, prepare for the day, eat breakfast, read scriptures, pray, and then work on the home. At noon my grandmother made a delicious meal for us to enjoy. Work would resume until the evening, and the sun would set. We would return home, have dinner, pray, and then rest for the next day.

I was not amused, but I obeyed. The Western culture part of my brain was telling me to have fun, be wild, and run free on this island paradise. However, the Tongan side of me, the voice of my mother, was reminding me of the importance of faka'apa'apa (respect) and fatongia (duty). I complied with his schedule without complaint.

During my stay, my grandfather insisted that I read the scriptures out loud in Tongan. It was a horrifying prospect for me. I could understand Tongan but had little interest in reading it, especially out loud. I obeyed. His patience during those early reading sessions must have been more painful for him than they were for me. It was slow, tedious, and frustrating to read scriptures in Tongan. These were old religious Tongan words, not conversational words. Still, we persisted every morning. He was exact in his teaching, and he expected me to improve. I did improve.

My grandfather still had duties at the Temple, so he assigned 'Inoke Mo'unga to accompany me to work on the home. Every morning 'Inoke would pick me up to work on the home. My grandfather finished his work in the Temple at noon, and then we would all work together until the early evening. 'Inoke was very kind. He taught me a lot about carpentry, and he helped me speak Tongan.

My favorite part of the day was lunch because it allowed my grandfather and me to have deep conversations. My grandfather would ask me doctrinal questions, and I would share my thoughts. He would listen and then help me see things in a new way. He taught me principles.

For example, he taught me that charity was the most important thing for anyone to possess. Then he asked me what I should do to develop charity. I guessed various things, but he would say, "no." Then he said, "The most im-

Eating lunch and discussing gospel topics in between work on the house.

portant thing you can do to develop charity is to work. Work for the Lord. Work to help people." This conversation was memorable to me because after he said those words, I looked up and marveled at the big vast, beautiful Tongan sky. A balmy wind was blowing, and there was such a feeling of peace. I did not want it to end.

Me and my grandmother Hēhea as she prepares food.

We worked on that home the entire time I was on the island, even though I longed to run around with friends. Once, one of my friends came to visit, and he asked if I could go with them. I admire the bravery of my friend Vaikalafi Lutui, Jr. because my grandfather could be an intimidating man. I was grateful he asked, but he was turned away.

As the summer lingered on, what I dreaded soon became what I enjoyed. I enjoyed reading the scriptures in Tongan with my grandfather. I loved our time talking. I looked forward to building the home with him. I even enjoyed watching him become frustrated when I did something wrong. He was a very articulate person. He paid attention to every detail. He inspected everything I did, and if it were not correct, we would start over. I learned quickly to take extra time to do it right the first time rather than trying to get things done quickly with minimal effort. He missed nothing. By the end of summer, the home almost finished. Only the finishing touches were left, and it was time for me to return home.

Leaving Tonga.

I remember the day I left Tonga (partly because my grandfather insisted, I wear a suit, yes, with a tie, on the flight home). Parting was difficult. I looked at the home we had built over the summer and realized just how much I had changed. I had learned new skills. I knew about carpentry. I felt healthier because I had been working. My Tongan language skills improved. We had built something durable and visible. It was something of real value. We created a house that would bless travelers who needed a place to stay while going to the Temple. I felt accomplished.

When I returned home to Utah, my life resumed, and soon friends and distractions interfered with things I had learned. I had forgotten. I continued with my life and did not think much about it until I returned to the house in 2015.

As I stood in front of this home with my daughter, the tears began to flow even more intensely as I realized my grandfather wasn't only building a home; he was building me. His work was to make me better. "Work. Work." I could hear his voice in my mind. He had built something that had outlasted his own life. I immediately wondered about what I was spending my life doing. What was my work? What was I doing? Then I realized, creating this book was a work I could do for him, after everything he had done for me.

The portrait I am sharing of my grandfather may be shocking to many who believe they knew him. The reality is, people are more complex than our singular interactions with them. To view my grandfather in only one specific way, usually that of a church leader, only allows us limited insight into him as a human. To me, he was a man, not a myth. He was wonderful, gifted, spiritual, and insightful, but still a man. He faced his life's challenges with faith and determination but who was human and had flaws (and he would agree) — a man who relied on the Lord. He was fiercely devoted to his wife — a family man above all.

Many in the Tongan community who associated with my grandfather knew him to be a strong-willed, no-nonsense, matter-of-fact kind of person. He would tell people bluntly, regardless of their feelings, the truth. He did not waste words or time. He demanded excellence from the people he worked with and expected them to be present and focused on the task at hand.

I have seen that side of him too. He could be demanding. Sometimes his correction could be considered harsh. Despite this, I knew whenever he gave me correction, it was because he loved me. I always knew he wanted what was best for me. Proverbs 13:24 reads, "He that spareth the rod hateth his son; but he that loveth him chasteneth him betimes." My grandfather corrected me because he loved me and did not want me to continue in error. I was grateful for that.

My grandfather's frankness is a strange trait to have as a Tongan. Tongan culture values fe' tokoni'aki (helping each other and getting along) and tauhi va (keeping relations) where maintaining peace is the ultimate goal. My grandfather was always more concerned about doing what was right than what was popular. It was his forwardness that endeared him to so many. No one had to guess where he stood on any topic because he would tell you. I have learned that there is comfort in that kind of honesty.

One side I wish people knew more about was his funny side. For example, while in Tonga as a teenager, I went with the ward youth group to perform temple baptisms. The ward failed to set the appointment up with the Temple, but that did not stop us. We showed up without notice as if it would be ok.

There were other groups there as well, so our appearance was not helpful to the temple staff. My grandfather was not pleased. He was a man of order. I remember him looking at us, dressed in white, ready to go, but with a backlog of other groups already there. Our ward leader apologized. Then I heard my grandfather say, "Malo pe oku mou ha'u ke mou si'i kaukau he uikeni." (Well, at least you will all have at least one bath this week.) I began to laugh, and he looked at me with a slight grin. We were allowed to do baptisms, and he even shook everyone's hand when we left.

His wit and humor were even funnier when he was with his wife, Hēhea. Hēhea's laugh was contagious. My grandfather always spoke kindly to my grandmother. They enjoyed being together.

My grandfather lived in Tonga, and I lived in Utah, so our interactions were limited. I feel as though this arrangement magnified my memories of him. Every experience was unique because every interaction was rare. Still, they visited the United States frequently and would stay with us for extended periods. Later in their lives, their visits would be longer. When I was older, I could drive them places. I would take my grandparents to medical appointments. My grandfather was meticulous about his health, especially later in life, after being diagnosed with diabetes.

How did I come to write this history?

I was fully aware of my grandfather's prominence among Tongan saints when I was a child. Tongans and papālangi would often recount miraculous events or things he had done that changed their lives. The stories were endless. I would listen, nod, and agree. To me, he was my grandfather. And the person I knew was much more beloved to me because of what he was, more than what he had done.

I know my grandfather wanted his history recorded since I was a young adult. The last time I visited him in his home in Tonga was in 1999. I remember seeing a table full of journals, pictures, and boxes of articles from his life. Sometimes he would show me specific things. During one of these moments, he said that everything he had was important information for the history of the church in Tonga. I believed him.

The image of those materials and his words haunted me for many years. My thought was always, "Well, if this is important for the history of the church in Tonga, then who is going to write it?" I imagined a scholar would appear and want to do it, so I waited. My waiting turned into impatience in 2001 when I wrote my grandfather a letter in Tongan requesting he bring all of his historical items to the United States to document his history. I discovered my letter among his things after his death and found it amusing. I was pushing (as is my way) to do this for years

When my grandfather passed away in 2002, I felt defeated. He was no longer here, but those boxes of historical items still existed. The materials remained in his home while my grandmother, Hēhea, was still living. She passed away in 2005, and my concern for my grandfather's history became even more worrisome. After both of their deaths, their home lay empty. Almost all of the descendants of Tonga Toutai and Hēhea had moved to the United States. I was worried. Papers and photos often decay in Tonga's extreme humidity. Fortunately, the Lord provided a way to preserve everything.

My mother, the eldest daughter of Tonga Toutai and Hēhea, was serving a mission in Tonga when my grandmother passed away. Before she returned to the United States, she stopped by her parents' home and packed up all the historical items. She filled one suitcase, filled another and then another. My mother paid additional fees to ship everything back to the United States.

Once the items arrived, my mother and I realized the volume of materials was overwhelming. It was more than overwhelming; it was paralyzing. Pictures, mostly unlabeled, some damaged from years of exposure to the elements, had to be sorted. Journal entries were scattered. He saved the programs from meetings with little information about their historical value. The journal entries were the most voluminous. There were binders of information covering everything from important events to everyday schedules. There was a lot to go through.

I began to strategize. I decided that instead of trying to tackle the entire lifetime, I would focus on one area of my grandfather's life. Doing one area at a time would be easier, and the work would be focused. I decided to work on his time as a Temple President.

The task was not easy. It required translation from Tongan to English, the organization of records, gathering pictures, and planning an outline. Luckily, my grandfather had prepared me for this. Reading the scriptures as a teenager with him during that summer inspired me to read Tongan literature throughout the years. I was prepared to do it because of his influence.

I pushed through, and in 2008, I completed a book about the building of the Tonga Temple. The book contained pictures of the construction of the Temple with excerpts from my grandfather's journals. At last, progress.

This book about the building of the Temple ended up in surprising places. Family members received the book, and a copy made its way to John H. Groberg. I then received a call from him asking me if I could give a copy to Elder Boyd K. Packer, then president of the Quorum of the Twelve Apostles. I was delighted to drop one off at his office. It was all arranged for me to take it into the building and leave it at the front desk. I was happy to do so.

When I arrived at the Church Administration Building, Elder Packer wanted to meet me. I was not prepared to meet him. My wife, my daughter, and I went to Elder Packer's office, and we visited with him for a while. He asked about the book and my grandfather. He told me they were "very dear friends" and that he "loved" Tonga Toutai (that's what he called him) very much." It was a touching opportunity for me to spend a short time with Elder Packer, a memory I would cherish for the rest of my life.

During this same time, my mother had returned to Tonga to serve another mission (this would be her sixth mission), and she was there for the rededication of the Tonga Temple. There she met Elder Russell M. Nelson and his wife, Wendy, who had come to officiate at the rededication. During their visit, my mother gifted him a copy of our book.

It was time to continue working on an expanded history, but I needed to find someone who could answer questions. It was clear I needed to talk to someone who knew and served with my grandfather. I turned to John H. Groberg.

In 2007 I traveled to Idaho Falls to interview President Groberg (he and Jean were serving as the Temple President and Matron). I brought a box of unlabeled pictures and some writings. We met for a few hours in their home. Ever the gracious host, he allowed me to tape-record our visit. There I learned more about my grandparents and their work in Tonga. President Groberg provided a very human side to my grandfather.

I began to formulate a timeline and put events into place. All of this information allowed me to start viewing my grandfather's life in chronological order. I was then able to look at outside resources to complete additional background information on events occurring in the Kingdom of Tonga and around the world. Combining this information gave me context into what was happening around him, who was there, and why certain things were important.

I have approached this work with a western (papālangi) mindset. I wanted to share my grandfather's life in the context of facts. Using his journals and writings as a foundation, I began to organize other written documents, videos, audio recordings, and interviews to reconstruct the events of his life. Included are references to Tongan history and worldwide cultural events to provide additional context to the reader. Everything has been evaluated and fact-checked with mission records and resources from the Church History Library. I have included references should future researchers wish to add to their projects. A chronology of events and additional notes on each chapter are also included to provide clarity for the reader. This work was not an exercise in romanticizing him but in revealing him as a person of his time. This book contains excerpts from his writings directly. I provide narration for clarity, but I tried to keep to his words and thoughts at the forefront. I attempted to document it in a straightforward manner that is easy to follow.

Because of this, I have been cautious about including some of the miraculous stories that occurred during his life. Stories that I have heard first hand from those that experienced them. Accounts that include blessing a childless couple with children, telling missionaries during a drought to drink the ocean water, and it would be sweet, healing the sick, dreams, and visions. There were even stories about Tonga Toutai arriving late to catch a flight, but telling the gate agent the flight would return to pick him up because he needed to be at a conference on another island. I decided to exclude most of these accounts for three reasons: first, because he would be the first to acknowledge it was the will of the Lord and not him. Second, there are too many stories to choose from, and third, some experiences are too tapu (sacred) to share openly.

I hope someone will take the time to document all of the miraculous stories. I hope this work inspires someone to build on my grandfather's life further. Just as we built a house together during my teen years, this should provide enough of a blueprint to continue adding to this work. I feel that many of those stories could be beneficial to future generations. I know it would be an invaluable record.

While this approach seems straight forward, I hope the reader keeps in mind the complexity of the Tongan culture that was, at times, challenging for Tonga Toutai. In many of his writings (and especially when he received a new calling), he often states, "there are many people against this." or "there are many people who disagree I should hold this calling." It's hard to imagine, but there always seemed to be strong opposition coming from within the culture. Fellow Tongans were murmuring he was "self-righteous," or that he was of low social rank, or that he wanted to be papālangi or any number of things that would have made lesser men stumble. To be a pāpalangi and a church leader was viewed more with acceptance because foreigners are outside of the confines of Tongan culture. For Tonga Toutai, bound by those cultural ties (and his worldview tied to the culture), it made him a target for ridicule and persecution. His writings contain in-depth articulations of the Holy Bible and Book of Mormon prophets, and their stories mirrored his own.

One benefit of being inside of the culture was his ability to maximize effectiveness with the Tongan saints. He knew them, understood them, and was one of them. He was able to understand their struggles and help them overcome them. For example, Tongans were notorious for not being on time. When Tonga Toutai was in charge of the Area Conference and the groundbreaking ceremonies for the Temple, he followed a tight schedule with little or no mishaps. As a stake president, he had 100% attendance at stake leadership meetings. These feats required him to be skillful at working with people to move the work forward. It was not a small task, but he found a way to motivate those he worked with to do what was needed. That is one of the reasons he is remembered so fondly by those who have worked with him. He was able to bring out the best in people.

When I left Tonga as a teenager, my sister sent me a letter that gave further insight into my grandfather. In the days following my departure, my grandfather would open the door of my room, stand in the doorway, and look in at the emptiness without saying a word. Then after a few minutes, he would close the door. After watching him do this for a few days, my sister asked him if he was all right. He would nod to her without saying a word. I understood what he was feeling. In 2015 I was standing in front of the house we built together when I was a teenager, and I had no words to say. I missed him.

There is a Tongan saying, *si'i kai ha* (small but appearing), which means that although someone may want to present something extravagant, it may not be practical or possible, so it is better to show up with something small than to not show up at all. Following my grandfather's counsel, this is my work. It is small, but it is here.

Siope Lee Kinikini

Siope and daughter, Ileina, in front of the home.

Acknowledgments

A special thanks to my mom, Tangiteina, and my aunt, 'Akesiu. Their insight into my grandparents during his early years has been invaluable. They are credited as co-authors because they corrected and guided this entire project.

I'm grateful to John and Jean Groberg for the insights into my grandfather. The written documentation they have provided as well as the personal interviews have been very helpful.

I owe a huge debt of gratitude to earlier writers who documented life in Tonga. Specifically to Eric B. Shumway and Tevita Mapa for their interviews with my grandfather during different stages of his life. Eric B. Shumway's book, *Tongan Saints: Legacy of Faith*, was particularly helpful. A special thanks to R. Lanier Britsch, who documented the history of the church in Tonga in his book, *Unto the Isles of the Sea*.

To the countless missionaries who kept records of the church in Tonga from the early 1900s forward. Their reports are found in the Church History Library. These records provided dates, locations, names and events that established the historical accuracy of this book.

A special thanks to Lorraine Morton for her pictures, information and constant devotion to Tonga and Tongans. Tongan saints owe a great debt to the Morton family. A special thanks to the Kakalosi Tuione family as well for their images.

I am grateful for my siblings, who proofread manuscripts and provided additional: Vika, Deanna, Sini, Tonga, Leilini, Milika, Salote, Salome. Thank you.

To Isileli Tupou and Ruth Kongaika for input and picture editing. Malo.

My deepest thanks goes to my wife, Liana, and daughter, Ileina, whose patience and encouragement kept this project alive until completion.

Chronology of events

The following section contains a brief summary of some of the chronological order of events of the Church of Jesus Christ of Latter-day Saints, Tongan history and the life of Tonga Toutai Pāletu'a. Information was compiled from church records and Tonga Toutai's own personal records. Tonga Toutai's history is indented for clarity.

1820	Joseph Smith receives a visitation from God the Father and Jesus Christ ushering in the restoration of the gospel.
1830	Joseph Smith organizes the Church of Jesus Christ.
1843	Joseph Smith sends four missionaries: Addison Pratt, Benjamin Grouard, Noah Rogers, Knowlton Hanks to share the gospel in Polynesia. They would be the first missionaries to speak a language other than English.
1891	July 15: Alva Butler and Brigham Smoot arrive in Tonga to open the Tonga District of the Samoa Mission.
1892	July 16: Missionaries visit King George Tupou I.
1895	First LDS meeting held in Vava'u.
1897	Tonga District of the Samoa Mission closes. All missionaries return to Samoa
1907	June 13: Elders Heber J. McKay and W.O. Facer arrive in Neiafu by invitation of 'Iki Tupou Fulivai. Missionaries return to Tonga. A small branch and school are established.
1911	July 15: King George II attends a Mormon baptism at Fanga'uta. Relations between the church and government is tenuous but improving
1916	The Tonga Mission is established.
1918	April 5: Queen Sālote ascends to the throne of Tonga. November: President Willard Smith conducts first mission wide conference in Tonga at Matavaimo'ui.

Chronology

1921	June 11-July 4: Apostle David O. McKay visits Tonga mission.
1922	The Passport Act is passed. Visa restrictions do not allow foreign LDS missionaries to enter Tonga.
1923	June 13: Tonga Toutai is born in Pangai, Ha'apai to Viliami and Milika Mafi Pāletu'a. He is the sixth of eleven children.
1924	July 3: Select stipulations of the Passport Act in Tonga is repealed. Previously only five Caucasian missionaries were serving. Allowance is granted for more foreign missionaries. Missionaries from Canada and the United States arrive the following year.
1929	May/June: Elder Floyd C. Fletcher organizes a Boy Scout Troup and begins teaching Tongans the principles of the scouting program.
	Tonga Toutai begins elementary school. He hears of the gospel from one of his teachers.
1932	Apostasy in the mission. Mission President Cutler accompanies his wife to Hawaii for medical care. He is unable to return to the mission. Four missionaries, (three foreign, one Tongan) lead the church into apostasy. It would take 15 months for a new mission president, President Wiberg, to arrive.
1935	Queen Sālote refuses to see the missionaries.
1936	Emile C. Dunn, accompanied by his wife, Evelyn Hyde Dunn arrive in Tonga with two children to replace President Wiberg.
1938	May 10: Apostle George Albert Smith and Seventy Rufus K. Hardy arrive for conferences; dedicate chapel in Neiafu and recreation hall in Ha'alaufuli. They also travel to Vava'u and Ha'apai. They visit with Queen Sālote. President Dunn asks Elder Morton to commence translation of the Book of Mormon into the Tongan language.
	Tonga Toutai's life is miraculously preserved from falling off of a horse.
1939	Elder Ermel J. Morton, assisted by Elder Lee, Elder Wilding, Tēvita Mapa and Tu'iketei Pule complete the first drafts of the translation of the Book of Mormon in the Tongan language. Elder Morton is released and takes the transcript back to Salt Lake City to the First Presidency in preparation for publication.
	Tonga Toutai attends Tonga College ('Atele) in Nuku'alofa, Tonga.

1940	October 15: President Dunn receives cablegram from the First Presidency. The message read, "Having in mind possible developments, please make necessary boat reservations and return all elders to the United States as soon as possible in American ships where available. We will try to facilitate reservations from this end. Install local officers to take charge of branches. Send elders in as large of groups as possible, properly organized and officered. We urge the strictest possible conduct and caution against political controversies. The president of the mission will remain for the present using his own discretion whether his family will remain with him or return now."
1941	Church conference held in Pangai. Church membership exceeds 2,000.
	Tonga Toutai returns home to Ha'apai in November after school ends for the year. He reunites with his family. He tells them he is going to be baptized a member of the Church of Jesus Christ of Latter-day Saints.
1942	Relief Society Centennial is celebrated in each island group. Twelve Tongan families are called to serve missions.
	American troops are stationed throughout Tonga.
	January 11. Tonga Toutai is baptized a member of the Church of Jesus Christ of Latter-day Saints.
1943	Tonga Toutai is set apart as a Deacon by Lisiate Talanoa Maile. Tonga returns to school to continue his education. His area of study is agriculture.
1944	Severe famine in Niuafo'ou. Church sends relief and aid.
1945	June 17 - Set apart as a Teacher in the Priesthood by 'Epalahame Tui'one
	Tonga Toutai begins training as an educator. He enters the Teaching College in Nuku'alofa.
1946	Tonga Toutai finishes Teaching College and is qualified to be a professional educator.
1947	February 4: Future foreign missionaries are limited by government policy. Allowance is given for only three foriegn missionaries, plus the mission president.

Chronology

	Matthew Cowley approves property for the construction of Liahona College.
	Tonga Toutai begins work as an assistant and teacher in the government school in Faleloa.
1948	Tonga Toutai moves toPangai, Ha'apai as a teacher. It was brief. In December, he returns to Tongatapu to work as a building missionary on the newly announced Liahona College.
	Tonga Toutai meets Lu'isa Hēhea Kona'ī.
1949	January 27: Tonga Toutai and Hēhea are married. Tonga Toutai receives the Melchizedek Priesthood and is called to serve as a missionary. He is set apart by President Dunn.
	Tonga Toutai meets the Apostle Matthew Cowley in Ha'afeva, Ha'apai.
	August 29: Matthew Cowley, with the assistance of Elders Mosese Muti and Reuben M. Flynn, lay the conerstones of Liahona College.
1950	First child is born. Tangiteina Lesieli Pāletu'a. She is born in Matahau, Tongatapu. Hehea and the baby stay with her family while Tonga Toutai is working as a headmaster in Ha'ano.
1951	Tonga Toutai's employment with the government Department of Education moves him to teach in Mo'unga'one.
	Second chid is born. She is named 'Akesiu Salome Pāletu'a.
1952	February 11: Liahona school opens. The staff consisted of several Tongan teachers and five foreign teaching missionaries. The government forbade Liahona teachers from proselyting.
	Employment with the government necessitates Tonga Toutai moving twice this year. Once to Hafoa for the first six months and then a transfer to Fahefa for the remaining six months.
1953	December 1: Liahona College is dedicated by Elder LeGrand Richards. Her Majesty, Queen Sālote attends the ceremony. Elder Richards is accompanied to Tonga by former mission president, Evon Huntsman.
1954	Employment with the government assigns Tonga Toutai to serve

	as headmaster, first in Talafo'ou for six months and then to Nomuka.
1955	Tonga Toutai is called to work at the new Liahona College by Ermel Morton and D'Monte Coombs. He resigns a secure post with the Deparment of Education inTonga to work in the newly formed Liahona College to fulfill his calling.
1956	Tonga Toutai travels to Melbourne, Australia as a representative of scouting in Tonga. *Additional note: It is unclear whether this trip was for the Scout Jamboree or for the 1956 World Olympics. Both of these events happened in Australia this year but only the Olympics occurred in Melbourne.
1957	Tonga Toutai works with Brother Manwaring overseeing affairs at Liahona.
1958	Tonga Toutai, Hēhea and their children travel to the New Zealand Temple with other Tongan families to receive temple ordinances. The family is sealed on December 31.
1959	Tonga Toutai is called as Second Counselor to President Viliami Sovea Kioa in the Hihifo District.
1960	Tongan translation of the Doctrine and Covenants and the Pearl of Great Price arrive in Tonga.
	March: Thirty-one Tongan labor missionaries travel to Hawaii to construct several new buildings at the Church College of Hawaii.
	October 26: The first seminary graduation at Liahona is held.
1961	April: Liahona College officially becomes Liahona High School
1962	Tonga Toutai is called to serve on the Mission Council under President Patrick Dalton.
1963	President Dalton asks Tonga Toutai to pray for rain during a conference in Vava'u because of severe drought. Before the end of the day a heavy rain had fallen.
1965	Called as District President in Hihifo.
	Queen Sālote passes away. Her son, Taufau'ahau takes her place. Mis-

sion president John H. Groberg and his wife are invited to the coronation ceremony.

1966	August 2: Called as a counselor in the Mission Presidency serving with President John H. Groberg.
1967	Tangiteina marries Pita Masaku Kinikini.
1968	September 5: The first stake in Tonga is organized. Tonga Toutai is called as a counselor in the first stake in Tonga. He is second counselor to President Orson White who was set apart by Elder Howard W. Hunter. He is ordained a High Priest by Thomas S. Monson.

Elder Thomas S. Monson observes Tonga Toutai teaching students at Liahona and learns the lesson of the makafeke.

Tonga Toutai and Hehea visit Salt Lake City for General Conference and they meet President David O. McKay. An invitation is extended to N. Eldon Tanner to attend the Jubilee celebration in Tonga. He agrees and attends the ceremonies in November.

October 2: Tonga Toutai receives his patriarchal blessing from church patriarch Eldred G. Smith in Salt Lake City.

1969	November 19: Tonga Toutai is called and ordained as a Patriarch by Legrand Richards for all of Tonga. Tonga Toutai is the first Tongan to hold this position. He records in his journal that he fasted all week in gratitude for this blessing. He also reported he was able to provide many patriarchal blessings during this time.
1970	Tonga Toutai and Hehea travel to Papeete (Tahiti), Acapulco (Mexico), Los Angeles (California) and Salt Lake City (Utah).

Tonga Toutai enrolls 'Akesiu in LDS Business college in Salt Lake City, Utah.

1971	July 20: Called to serve as the Stake President for the Hihifo (West) Stake. Elders Howard W. Hunter and Groberg are present for the stake organization.
1973	'Akesiu marries Tevita Mapa Vainuku in the Salt Lake Temple.

October 8: Tonga Toutai receives a letter from President Harold B. Lee, the prophet of the church describing his "unusual leadership skills in guiding the members of his stake to fulfill their responsibilities.

1974	May 5: Tonga Toutai is called to serve as the Mission President of the Tonga Nuku'alofa Mission. He is set apart by Elder Thomas S. Monson and Elder John H. Groberg on May 21.
	Sister Pāletu'a works with church leaders to institute a missionary dress code. There are official guidelines for elders and sisters regarding their dress.
1975	Jan 4: Tonga Toutai blesses land in Vava'u for a school. This school becomes Saineha High School.
	December 25: Conference for missionaries called the "White Christmas" which was a year long effort to teach and baptize.
	December: Tonga Toutai has an article in the LDS Church Ensign magazine with the title, "I Couldn't Hold Back the Tears."
1976	Jan 5: "Ta'u oe Kau Leimana" (Year of the Lamanite) is the mission theme. Missionary work grows.
	Area Conference is held in Tonga with visiting Church Leaders arriving in Tonga with the prophet, Spencer W. Kimball. Tonga Toutai is in charge of organizing the conference.
	November 19: Meeting with King Taufa'ahau IV and Elder John H. Groberg.
1977	April 28: Elder Bruce R. McConkie and Tonga Toutai travel to Vava'u for conferences.
	May 5: Tonga Toutai is called as a Regional Representative of the Twelve Apostles in the Tonga region.
	June: The Kingdom of Tonga has a major earthquake.
	October 5: While visiting Salt Lake City for General Conference, Tonga Toutai is set apart by Elder Marion D. Hanks and Elder John H. Groberg as Regional Representative for the Twelve Apostles. Attending were his wife, Hehea and Tangteina.
1978	March 29: The First Presidency expands Tonga Toutai's responsibilities from the Tonga region and now includes the Tahiti region.
1980	April 2: The Church officially announces a temple to be built in Nu-

ku'alofa Tonga during General Conference.

Tonga Toutai is told of the Temple before the worldwide announcment and is called to organize the groundbreaking ceremonies.

1981	December 1: Official release date as a Regional Representative of the Twelve Apostles.
1982	September 21: Tonga Toutai is set apart to be the Temple President of the Tonga Temple. They attend the Temple President's Seminar in Salt Lake City, Utah on September 28-30.
1983	Ha'apai Stake is divided. The Kindom of Tonga has ten stakes.
1985	January 2: Speech given at the Tongan Palace at 3:00. Tonga Toutai does something unusual which may be construed as culturally inappropriate. Tongan custom dictates that all people should be physically lower than the king and royalty. Tonga Toutai delivers his remarks standing. His remarks are focused on church growth in the islands and a desire to make Tonga an "Eden" in the pacific.
1989	August 25: Tonga Toutai is called as the President of the Missionary Training Center in Tonga.
1990	Feb 1: The Tonga Missionary Training Center is dedicated.
1992	Centennial celebration of the church in Tonga is held in various locations around the world. Tonga Toutai participates in the celebration in Tonga.
	Tonga Toutai continues to serve in the temple and as a patriarch.
1995	June 3: Grandson Pāletu'a Nukuluve Vainuku passes away from injuries sustained while playing rugby. He is buried in a family plot near the Temple. Tonga Toutai names the plot area, Nukuluve.

Celebration honoring Pioneers of the Pacific held at Brigham Young University-Hawaii. Tonga Toutai and Hēhea attend. They meet many friends and acquaintances including Elder Rodney Komatsu and President Gordon B. Hinckley.

2002	December 15: Tonga Toutai passes away during his sleep at home in Matangiake, Tongatapu. He is buried at the family plot near his grandson, Nukuluve.
2005	May 16: Hēhea passes away in Hawaii. She is returned to Tongatapu and rests with her husband.

Genealogy

Tonga Toutai and Hēhea Family

Tonga Toutai and Hēhea had two children.

Tangiteina Lesieli	'Akesiu Salome
(Pita Masaku Kinikini)	(Tevita Mapa Vainuku)
Vika Fatafehi	Seini
Hēhea Lu'isa	Tonga
Siope Lee	Soana
Deanna Vai	Mapa Jr.
Jean Roseglen	Hēhea
Tonga Toutai	'Ilavalu
Leilini Viliami	Nukuluve Pāletu'a
Milika Mafi	Kaunanga Metuloni
Salote Marie	Sosaia
Salome 'Akesiu	Maluofi
	Vikia
	Salome

Viliami Pāletu'a/Milika Mafi Family Ancestry

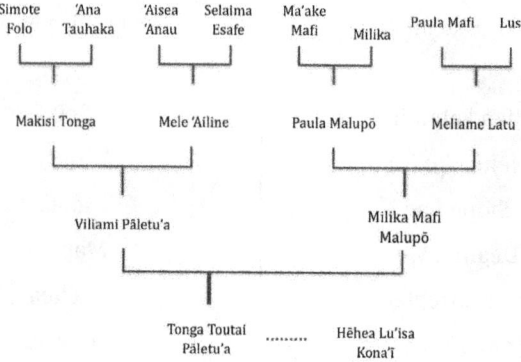

Viliami and Milika Mafi Pāletu'a Family

The children of Viliami and Milika Mafi are listed in birth order.

(1) Penisimani Langoia 'i Pangai (m)

(2) 'Uikilifi Mafi (m)

(3) 'Ulamoleka (m)

(4) Sione Masalu (m)

(5) Mele Hu'avai (f)

(6) Tonga Toutai (m)

(7) 'Ana Tauhaka (f)

(8) Tevita Faioso (m)

(9) Lu'isa Malama (f)

(10) Akanesi Manuna (f)

(11) 'Uaisele Tangilapa (m)

Kona'i Family Ancestry

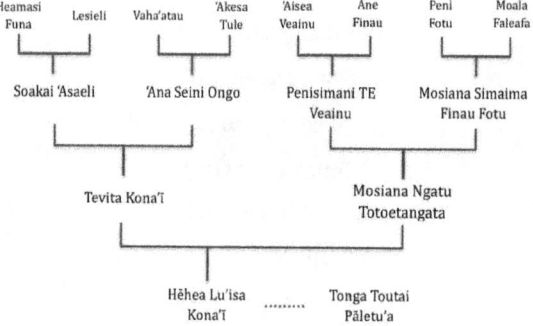

Maps of Tonga

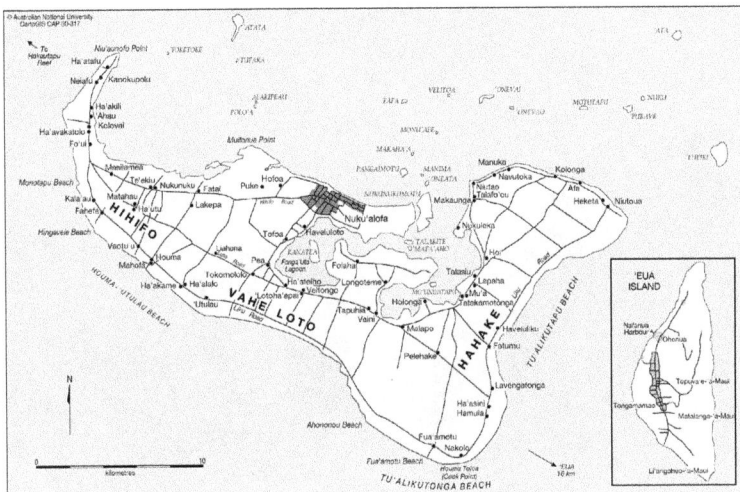

Tongatapu: Tongatapu is the largest island in the southernmost group of islands in the Kingdom of Tonga. It is divided into three districts: Western (Hihifo), Central (Vaheloto), and Eastern (Hahake).

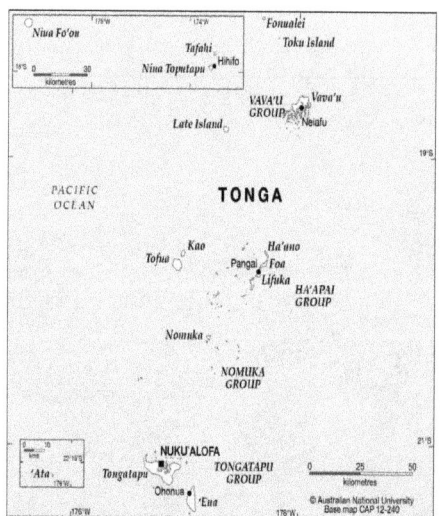

The Kingdom of Tonga consists of three island groupings.

Tongatapu is located in the south where, Nuku'alofa, the capital city is located. The group to the group to the north is known as the Ha'apai Group. Further north is the Vava'u Group.

There are roughly 169 islands that comprise the Kingdom of Tonga, however, only 36 are inhabited.

Chapter 1

Beginnings | 1923 - 1939

But great are the promises of the Lord unto them who are upon the isles of the sea; wherefore as it says isles, there must needs be more than this, and they are inhabited by our brethren.
Jacob 10:21

A New World

In 1923, the world was beginning anew. The end of World War I signaled a time of invention and progression. The year 1923 would include the following advancements: discovery of King Tutankhamen's tomb in Egypt, development of the first portable radio in the United States, the selling of the first domestic refrigerator in Sweden, and the introduction of insulin to treat diabetes in Canada.

On the other side of the world on a small South Pacific island, Tonga Toutai Pāletu'a was born in Pangai, Ha'apai, on June 13, 1923.

The Pāletu'a Family

Tonga Toutai's father, Viliami Pāletu'a, was a descendant of a noble family from the small island of Mo'unga'one, in the Lifuka District of Ha'apai. Mo'unga'one is small. Only 1.17 km square in size and a population of around 100 people. While the Pāletu'a family had noble status in Mo'unga'one, the family moved to the larger, more populated city of Pangai, Ha'apai. Viliami worked as a *faifekau* (minister) for the Church of Tonga.

Viliami's family were nobles on the small island of Mo'unga'one. There is a family story that Viliami wanted to move back to Mo'unga-one, but Milika refused, so the family remained in Pangai. Moving back to a small island could have provided the comforts of nobility, but the family would have access to more resources by staying in the more populated area of Pangai.

Viliami and Milika Pāletu'a enjoyed a close relationship with Milika Mafi's side of the family. Tonga Toutai would often stay with Milika's brother, Fetuani, during his youth. Milika's sister, Melenaite, passed away in 1918, and her daughter, Fepaki, was a raised (*pusiake*) by Viliami, and Milika. They raised her as their daughter, and Tonga Toutai always referred to her as his sister. There are no records of how Melenaite died; however, she passed away at the height of the *mahaki faka'auha*, also known as the "Spanish flu." The devastation from the Spanish flu wiped out over 100 million people around the world and in the kingdom of Tonga, an estimated 8% of the population. Fepaki would later move to Nuku'alofa and marry Mafi Vaka.

Viliami and Milika Mafi Pāletu'a

Viliami and Milika were married in Pangai, Ha'apai, in 1910. Information about Viliami and Milika's courtship and marriage are unknown; however, arranged marriages were not uncommon. They were the parents of eleven children: Pensimani, 'Uikilifi Mafi, 'Ulamoleka, Sione Masalu, Mele Hu'avai, Tonga Toutai, 'Ana Tauhaka, Tēvita Faioso, Lu'isa Malama, 'Akanesi Manunā, and 'Uaisele Tangilapa. Seven boys, four girls. Tonga Toutai was the sixth of their eleven children.

In addition to their noble family line, Viliami and Milika Mafi were *faifekau's* (ministers) in the Church of Tonga. Their role as *faifekau's* would further elevate their standing in the community. In Tonga, *faifekau's* are revered and honored.

Early Life

Tonga Toutai's early life was simple.

> I was very healthy as I was growing up. My parents attended the Church of Tonga. When I was a baby, there was a boil inside my mouth, and to this day, you can still see a scar to my face and mouth. My favorite activities

The Paletu'a Family. Standing: 'Ana Tauhaka, Tevita Faioso, Lu'isa Malama. Sitting, left to right: Viliami Paletu'a, Siosifa Kulitapa (son of 'Ana Tauhaka) and Milika Mafi.

were playing Cricket, playing marbles, flying kites, and best of all, swimming in the sea (Mapa 1).

He attended church every week, where his father preached. He writes, "My parents and entire family were of the Church of Tonga." Tonga Toutai grew up in a home that was centered on the word of the Lord.

Tongan *faifekau's* are dynamic orators. Gifted in the art of persuasive reasoning, and knowledgable with the scriptures, Tongan *faifekau's* deliver their sermons with power. It is common to hear a Tongan *faifekau* raise their voice, pound a pulpit, exclaim scriptures and speak in measured tempos to emphasize essential passages. As Viliami preached the gospel from the Holy Bible every week, young Tonga Toutai would watch with absorbed attention.

Memorizing scriptures would be expected in the Pāletu'a home. Tongans during the 1920s relied heavily on the ability to memorize important information. Family genealogies, Tongan history, scriptural passages, and essential events were passed down by oral tradition. The ability to recite important information at any moment is still a skill that is highly valued among the Tongan people. Tonga Toutai would pass the importance of memorizing scriptures to his children and grandchildren.

In 1929, at the age of six, Tonga Toutai began his formal education.

> I started primary school. These were the days of no paper and pencil, only hard slates and hard chalk. The headteacher was Tēvita Finau Tafuna assisted by Kesaia Funaki and Fifita 'Okoa. Other teachers were Sione Hu'akau, Malakai Lomu Tuiono, and Lupeni Fakahua.
>
> Tēvita Finau Tafuna was a prominent Latter-day Saint in Ha'apai with a booming voice and personality. He preached about the church even in school, so by the time I entered Tonga College in 1939, I had an understanding about the LDS Church, especially the need to be baptized by immersion (Shumway 209).

Tēvita Finau Tafuna was Tonga Toutai's first introduction to the Church of Jesus Christ of Latter-day Saints. The influence of his early teachers made a powerful impression on him and would inspire him to become a teacher.

Tonga Toutai was a good student. He had a talent to absorb information and teach it clearly to others. In addition to this, he was also able to observe his father using the skills of public speaking and persuasion as he preached every week. What he learned during these early years of his life prepared him for opportunities to serve in unique ways.

While education in Tonga was encouraged, a student would only progress dependent on their ability to pass exams. If a student failed their exams, they usually returned home to work on the family farm, fish, or find other employment. The primary purpose of education was to increase literacy among Tongans, but how much further a person progressed in their education would depend on their test scores. Only students with an aptitude for learning would continue to higher education.

Apostasy in Tonga

On August 17, 1932, mission president, Newel J. Cutler, left Tonga to take his wife, Floy, to receive medical treatment in Hawaii. When he arrived in Hawaii, he learned her condition was so weak that he would be unable to return to Tonga to complete his missionary duties. The missionaries in Tonga were without a leader.

A new mission president needed to be sent to care for the work and the missionaries still in Tonga. Finding someone to replace President Cutler took some time to find and then for travel. It took nearly fifteen months before the new mission president, Reuben M. Wiberg, arrived in Tonga. When he did, the mission and church were in near apostasy. Four missionaries, three Americans and one Tongan, had not only led members of the church astray, but they also disregarded the covenants they had made. There was discord among church members and unfavorable perceptions of the "Mormons" to Tongans. The damage was profound. The three foreign missionaries were excommunicated and sent back to the United States. The Tongan missionary was also excommunicated, but he repented and eventually returned to full fellowship.

Faithful members and missionaries persisted in working to repair relationships and share the gospel, but the work was difficult. A member of the church at the time stated, "most of the missionaries were sent home without finishing their missions. Because of this, there was much persecution towards the church by the non-members and the inactive members" ('Alatini-Richter 60).

The negative reputation of the church also affected relationships with the monarchy years later. The Tonga Nuku'alofa Mission report documented that on March 8, 1935, Elders Sosaia Tonga and Simote Fusitua tried to visit Queen Sālote at the palace, but they were not admitted. Queen Sālote "very emphatically stated that she had no time for a hearing with any Mormon except pertaining to governmental affairs" ("Tonga" 1:1:301).

Despite the difficulties, the Lord was sending new missionaries to build the kingdom. In May of 1935, three missionaries arrived in Tonga to begin the work again. Elders Thomas F. Whitley, Donald N. Anderson, and Floyd C. Fletcher worked hard to serve the Lord and gain the trust of the people and members of the church.

It would take years before perceptions about the church would change. In some places, it would not change. Not only was the Mormon church unfavorably viewed by the monarchy, the culture now saw it as immoral. The climate of religious tension would have been of particular interested to Viliami, Milika, and the entire Pāletu'a family. The need for saving souls was taught with more fervency during sermons, and the family was at the forefront of a spiritual war to save souls. The Mormons, for some Tongans, and especially the leaders of other religions, were dangerous.

Teen Years

Tragedy hit the Pāletu'a family in 1936 when Tonga Toutai's brother, Sione Masalu, suddenly died. He was seventeen years old. The cause of his death is unknown. Tonga Toutai and Sione were only a few years apart. Tonga Toutai was only thirteen years old when Sione passed away. The reality of mortality came to Tonga Toutai at a young age.

Tonga Toutai recorded the following experience in 1938 when he was 15 years old.

> My mother sent me to the plantation to get the *lo'akau* (to make mats) and put in the ocean. As I went, I fell from the horse. Perhaps I was dead for about two hours. They took me to Fetuani's home to stay. He only had one daughter, Meliame Latu. I noticed my uncle left his wife and was with another woman (Pāletu'a, diary).

The sudden passing of Sione Masalu and Tonga Toutai's own experience with death influenced his desire to understand his mortality and the things of eternity. Why was he preserved? Why did his brother die? What was the purpose of life? What happens after death? Tonga Toutai wanted to know. Later in life, Tonga Toutai would say he felt the Lord preserved his life for a specific purpose.

His observation about his uncle leaving his wife for another woman also made an impression on him. It indicated an early understanding of right and wrong.

Missionaries were visiting every home in Tonga, and they eventually made it to the Pāletu'a family. One day, when Viliami Pāletu'a was away, the missionaries came to the Pāletu'a home, and Tonga Toutai invited them inside. The missionaries shared their message. During the visit, Viliami returned home and was enraged to find the Mormon missionaries in his home. He chased them away, and Tonga Toutai was disciplined for inviting them into the home. Viliami forbade his son from inviting the missionaries to their home. Viliami also banned his son from associating with the Mormons.

Something intrigued Tonga Toutai about the missionaries, and he sought ways to hear their message. As a teenager, Tonga Toutai would find out where the missionaries would preach, and he would go to the meeting, but he would sit at a distance. This allowed him to hear the sermons without appearing like he was part of the group. Tonga Toutai learned about the restoration of the gospel, Joseph Smith. The account of Joseph Smith and his desire to know the truth resonated with Tonga Toutai (Kinikini "Teina Interview").

During this time, Tonga Toutai learned that the missionaries were working on translating The Book of Mormon into the Tongan language. A young missionary from Mapleton, Utah, Elder Ermel Morton, would lead the translation efforts with help from native Tongan church leaders. Translation began in 1938. The first draft would be completed in 1939. This draft was sent to Salt Lake City, Utah, to the First Presidency for review. Unfortunately, the Crown Prince of Tonga returned from Australia with a desire to formalize the written Tongan language. The Tongan translation of the Book of Mormon would not be completed until 1946.

Leaving Home

In the late 1930s and early 1940s, there were only five high schools in the kingdom of Tonga, and all five were located on the main island of Tongatapu. Four of the five were boarding schools. Each school served different groups of students; one for Methodist girls, one for Methodist boys, a government school for boys only, and a Seventh Day Adventist School for boys and girls. The fifth school as a Catholic school that provided classes only during the day, and it only allowed Catholic students (Koloi). Different religious groups sponsored four of the five High Schools. Only one school was non-denominational, the College of Tonga.

In 1939, at the age of sixteen, Tonga Toutai left home to attend High School in Nuku'alofa at the College of Tonga.

> I took exams for the College of Tonga (in 1941, the name of the college would be changed to 'Atele), which is the government school located in Nuku'alofa. In January, I entered the College of Tonga. I sailed to Tonga and stayed in Nuku'alofa. I lived with Fepaki Vaka and Mafi Vaka. Fepaki is my sister. The daughter of my mother's oldest sister. Her mother died, and Mafi was adopted by my parents. She came to Tonga and married with Mafi Vaka, and when I arrived, I stayed with them and attended school (Pāletu'a, diary).

There are no records of whether Tonga Toutai's older siblings attended school in Tongatapu; however, his writings indicate he went alone.

Schoolmates and Church

> It was in school that I met Teiko Fonua. In the large open space housing, our beds were next to each other. He was Mormon. We became great friends. My aunt and uncle told me to go to the Church of England because that was their church. I went to it, and I would go with Teiko and Vili Pasi also to the Mormon church in Matavaimo'ui.
>
> I was involved in sports. The dorms were divided into houses. The houses were named after the royals: Ngu, Tukeiaho, Taufa'ahau. I belonged to the house of Ngu.
>
> I would always go to Matavaimo'ui, and the teacher was Sulia Tu'iketaipule and a lady named Hola. On the weekends, we would go to Houma to Teiko's family, and we would attend the Mormon church.
>
> I worked as a house boy to Nikolasi Fonua. He was my third teacher at College (Mapa 1).

Moving to the main island of Tongatapu provided Tonga Toutai opportunities to associate with members of the church. At school, Tonga Toutai became school friends with Nomani Havili, Sitani Niupalau, and Viliami Pasi, all of whom spent time fellowshipping him. These friendships would last their lifetime, and Tonga Toutai considered them part of his family. Tonga Toutai became an active part of the "Mormon" church without actually being a member.

Testimony

With an already deep understanding of the Bible from his father, Tonga Toutai continued to learn more about the restoration of the gospel. However, it was the doctrine of priesthood authority that intrigued him most. The need for baptism by immersion by Priesthood authority. His natural curiosity and aptitude for learning pushed him to ask questions and seek understanding. He believed that living prophets should exist and that God still speaks to his children. He devoured what was available at the time, which was limited. His inquisitive nature kept him pondering and debating. Fortunately, Teiko Fonua was close at hand. Teiko, a fun-loving, happy person, was someone Tonga Toutai trusted. Teiko, in particular, was influential in helping Tonga Toutai learn more about the gospel. The more Tonga Toutai explored, the more he knew the gospel was true.

Tonga Toutai decided to become a member of the Church of Jesus Christ of Latter-day Saints in 1939. There was only one thing left to do. He needed to return home and tell his parents he was leaving their church and joining the "Mormons."

Chapter 2

Conversion | 1940 - 1949

Train up a child in the way he should go: and when he is old, he will not depart from it.
Proverbs 22:6

World War II

World War II reached the shores of Tonga. Soon the island was filled with foreign soldiers, and by the time they left in 1942, Tonga was never the same. The war introduced currency and materialism. This change altered Tongan culture indefinitely (Wood-Ellem 210). During the war years, soldiers took over the capital city of Nuku'alofa, and Tongans were asked to move inland. Even the mission home was surrendered to accommodate officers of war. A curfew was instituted, and lights or fires were not allowed at night. Despite the restrictions, members of the church would still hold meetings in the thick brush ("Tonga" 1:2:145).

Church President Heber J. Grant sent a telegram to mission president Emil C. Dunn and requested that all foreign missionaries return home. On October 24, 1940, all foreign missionaries serving in Tonga left the country, many to Hawaii. The prophet was inspired. The following year, on December 7, 1941, Pearl Harbor was attacked, and the United States officially joined the war.

Although all the missionaries left Tonga, President Dunn requested to stay behind. He did not want to leave the people and the work he loved. The progression of the work in Tonga had become more stable since the issues with apostate missionaries a few years earlier. The growth remained steady, and President Dunn feared what might happen if the members were left without priesthood leadership. Permission was granted, and President Dunn, his wife, and his family remained in Tonga. The responsibility of missionary work and of running the branches in the islands fell on President Dunn and the faithful Tongan saints. His sacrifice ensured the church would survive the war and that Tongan members could capably fill leadership roles in the future.

Return Home and Baptism

During his time at 'Atele, Tonga Toutai had been active in the Ha'ateiho and Matavaimo'ui branches and had developed a strong relationship with Teiko Fonua. His testimony continued to develop. He knew the church was true and was strengthened by the support of friends and church members. Now he just needed to return home and tell his parents.

Tonga Toutai had options on how to proceed with baptism. He could have been baptized while at school without his parent's knowledge. He could have stayed at school and notified his parents by letter. He could have started a new life without telling his parents at home in Pangai. Tonga Toutai chose to return home, tell his parents, and face the consequences. He wanted to be baptized at home. It was a bold decision but the right one. He had been raised by goodly parents who taught him to do things the right way. Letting his parents and family know about his decision and facing them despite the outcome was the right thing to do.

When the school year ended in November of 1941, Tonga Toutai sailed home to Pangai, Ha'apai. The voyage from Tongatapu to Pangai, Ha'apai, is a long one, a day to complete by boat. The journey would make stops to varying ports and islands along the way.

One can only imagine his thoughts

Travel throughout the kingdom of Tonga could take a few hours to a few days depending on where the boat was traveling, how many passengers, items being transported, weather and anticipated stops on neighboring islands along the way. Three boats serviced trips from Vava'u and Ha'apai to Nuku'alofa every week during the 1930-40's (Koloi).

while traveling home. Specifically, the thought of how his parents would react to his decision. Would they be angry? Would they be disappointed? Would he be disowned? Perhaps there was a belief that he could convince them of the truth. Perhaps.

Tonga Toutai reunited with his family in December of 1941. It was during this visit home that he told them he wanted to be baptized into the Church of Jesus Christ of Latter-day Saints. He was joining the *Mamongas* or Mormons.

His announcement was met with anger. It pained them to see their son reject their beliefs. It was the faith they had nurtured in their young son since his birth with the hope of guiding him toward God. To them, he was now forsaking them, and even worse, he was abandoning God.

The severity of the situation was further complicated because Tonga Toutai was not only joining a different church; he was joining the "Mormon" church. The same church the monarchy placed restrictions on a few years earlier — the same church where missionaries had led their members into apostasy and corruption. Tonga Toutai's decision went against everything they believed. As parents, they mourned for their son and worried about his soul. Discussions, pleadings, crying, and arguments followed in an attempt to dissuade him, but those attempts failed.

Tonga Toutai was undeterred. He knew the church was true, and he wanted to be a part of it. Despite the feelings of his parents, siblings, friends, and extended family, he was determined to be baptized. His baptism was scheduled in January.

Tonga Toutai writes the following about his baptism:

> On January 11, 1942, I was baptized to the LDS church in Lifuka by Taufu'i Tuione. The Holy Ghost was given to me by Kelepi 'Ikatauimoana La'iafi. I could hear the screaming and the yelling from a crowd, "Die! Drown!" Even though it was hard to hear, it didn't pierce my soul to what I knew to be true.
>
> From then, I moved from my house (Pāletu'a, journal).

Later in his life, Tonga Toutai gave a more detailed account of his baptism with his trusted friend, Elder John H. Groberg. Decades later, it was shared in Elder Groberg's book, "Fire of Faith." This experience would be depicted in the movie, "The Other Side of Heaven 2: Fire of Faith".

> In anger or desperation or both, he (Tonga Toutai's father) told his oldest son to 'teach Tonga a lesson.' Encouraged by his father and drunken with anger, Tonga's older brother got a large stick and headed for the

beach. He arrived at the beach just as the baptism was finished and as Tonga and the two elders were wading back to shore. In an anger-emboldened rage, he uttered a blood-curdling scream and headed straight toward the threesomes who were now in fairly shallow water. The two elders heard the scream, looked up, saw the stick and the charging brother, and quickly ran away. They yelled at Tonga to follow them, but he quietly shook his head and simply stood there, his eyes full of peace. He raised his head and looked straight at his brother. The elders reached land and took cover in some nearby bushes just before the brother reached Tonga. When his brother saw that Tonga would not run but waited calmly for him with a look of perfect serenity, he hesitated for a moment, but only a moment. Then with a curse of anger, he took the last couple of splashing steps, lifted his large stick, and sent it crashing across Tonga's back. Tonga still did not move. Again, and again, the stick smashed into his back, tearing his shirt and exposing huge red welts oozing with blood and pain.

At last, an extra heavy blow crumpled him to his knees, then another and another left him sprawled face down in the water. An exultant cry rent the air, and the enraged brother staggered to shore and disappeared uncertainly down the trail. He had "taught Tonga a lesson" and left a seemingly lifeless form floating partially submerged in the gently rolling ocean.

The two elders who had witnessed all this came from their hiding places and ran quickly to where Tonga lay in the ocean, barely moving. They were grateful to see he was still breathing. They lifted him from the water and were sickened by what they saw. Getting beaten severely enough to raise welts and blood and tear fabric is painful enough, but to have that raw flesh submerged in salty ocean water and sand was more pain than they could comprehend. They shuddered. They wondered whether Tonga also had some broken bones or other unseen injuries. Tonga could hardly move, so they each took an arm, lifted him up and dragged him stumblingly to shore.

As they got well onto land, Tonga spoke for the first time and asked where they were going. 'To the hospital, of course,' they replied. 'We must get those wounds treated and see if there are any broken bones. You may have some serious back or rib problems.'

"No," said Tonga. "Not yet. I have only been baptized. I have not received the gift of the Holy Ghost nor been confirmed a member of The Church of Jesus Christ of Latter-Day Saints-God's kingdom on earth. See that log over there? Take me to it, let me sit down, then confer upon me the gift of the Holy Ghost, and confirm me a member of the church. I want to be a full part of God's kingdom now."

'We'll do that tomorrow. You need to get some medical treatment now."

"No." Tonga replied firmly, "Do it now. Who knows, you may be right, there may be serious physical problems, I may not even make it to the hospital, or I may not be alive tomorrow. I am in pain, but mostly, I just feel numb. I am, however, in full control of my feelings, and I want to become a full member of God's kingdom now-please."

The two elders looked around, sensing possible danger. They saw no one else. They sat him down on the log, laid their hands on his head, and by the power and authority of the priesthood of God gave him the gift of the Holy Ghost, confirmed him a member of the Church of Jesus Christ of Latter-Day Saints and under the inspiration of God gave him a special blessing that no permanent physical damage from the beating would afflict him.

As they took their hands from his head, there was calmness in their eyes- no more furtive glances at the surrounding bushes, only tears of gratitude for the faith of a committed Tongan Saint in these latter days. Finally, they got him to the hospital, where he was checked, given some care, and released with admonition: "You were lucky this time. You have no life-threatening injuries or broken bones, but don't get into a fight like that again." (The doctor was not aware of the details.)

Tonga stayed with the elders that night, but the next day he wanted to return to his home. They went with him and found his father, who, still filled with bitterness and anger, commanded him to leave and never return. Tonga's older brother was nowhere to be found. The missionaries made arrangements for Tonga to live with member families (Groberg "Fire of Faith" 106-111).

Tonga Toutai had left his family to join the church of God.

Education, Teacher Training and Work

Tonga Toutai returned to Tongatapu and completed schooling at 'Atele. He records:

> I soon returned to 'Atele. In 1943 I continued school. One of my jobs in the school was to care for the horses. I also stayed in the home of Mafi and Fepaki Vaka. On December 27, 1943, I was ordained a Deacon by Lisiate Talanoa Maile of Nukunuku.
>
> It was at this time I made acquaintance with Mosese Muti, the branch president of Ha'ateiho, and a much-loved leader in the Church (Mapa 2; Shumway 210).

He next enrolled in the Teacher Training School in Nuku'alofa to become certified as an educator.

> I was selected to be a member of the first class of newly established Teacher Training College with Reverend Cecil F. Gribble of the Wesleyan Church as headmaster. I remained at school from 1944 to 1945. I played rugby at school. On Sundays, I would attend the Ha'ateiho Branch (Mapa 2; Shumway 210).

After the successful completion of his training, he was qualified as an educator. He immediately began working for the government of Tonga. These assignments usually lasted six months to a year. It also involved traveling to various islands.

Tonga Toutai as a young man

> My first teaching assignment after graduation was in the primary school in Faleloa, Ha'apai. The headteacher there at that time was Tupou' Ahofaiva Malekamu, an active Latter-day Saint (Shumway 210).

During this time, Tonga Toutai gained a deep understanding of the church in different parts of the kingdom of Tonga. In his first area of Faleloa, he stated the following about the branch:

> The fledgling branch of the Church in Faleloa in 1945 was sus-

tained largely by the faith and force of four women, Lupe Teutau, Taina Fonua, Pesi Hafoka, and Moala Makaafi.

The Tongan women of the branch in Faleloa had resilient faith. Tonga Toutai relates the following story in Eric B. Shumway's book, *Tongan Saints: Legacy of Faith*.

> I remember that Lātū Makaafi made a lot of fun of his wife and the other ladies for their faithfulness in the church. In fact, he had heard about their weekly fasts and would often follow them secretly into the bush where they met to pray. Then he and Tupou Malekamu would retreat and wait for them to come back from their devotions, at which time he would jeer at them and say, "We know what you are up to. You're fasting for us to join the church. We will never join, so spare yourselves the hunger."
>
> Well, the first thing you know, Tupou Malekamu was baptized. It was a beautiful service...
>
> Lātū Makaafi was there announcing that no way was he ever going to follow his wife into the church. To make his point, he raised his right hand and swore to heaven, it would never happen. He then raised his left hand and made the same "solemn" gesture while repeating his announcement. Then, as if this oath wasn't convincing enough, he sat down and lifted both his feet up (in ridicule, no doubt) and swore a covenant that he would never, never join the church. Well, he was baptized a few days later and has become a significant leader in the church. (Shumway 210-211)

His exposure to different people and areas of Tonga allowed him to understand the needs of the church. He also became familiar with members of the church throughout the kingdom. Traveling and working also allowed him to meet church leaders from Utah. In 1947 Tonga Toutai reported the following:

> I met Apostle Matthew Cowley in Ha'a'feva on the boat called Tu'iakitau. One of the apostles. (Mapa 3)

Despite a busy traveling and working schedule, he still found time to serve in callings. In 1948 he served as the President of the Sunday School for the District of Pangai. In December of that year, he was called to serve for two months as a building missionary for the a new high school, Liahona College. This calling involved shoveling sand during the day and proselyting with the other building missionaries at night. Tonga Toutai stated this time of his life was a joy.

Chapter 2

Courtship and Marriage

Tonga Toutai and Hēhea first met in Haʻapai in 1949. Hēhea traveled to Haʻapai with her sisters, Siale and Tangivale, to visit their brother Pīliote who was serving a mission.

Upon meeting Tonga Toutai, she did not think anything about a relationship but thought he was a kind man. Hēhea shares the following about their marriage:

> I shortly returned to Tongatapu. Tonga Toutai came to Tongatapu because he was teaching. Then one night, he came with a school friend from ʻAtele and attended a dance in Matahau (that is Hēhea's village). We danced together. Another young man saw us and told me that he did not think we should be dancing together.
>
> After the dance, he (Tonga Toutai) said to me, "Hea, I want to go and speak with your father and your mother."

It was apparent to Hēhea early on that Tonga Toutai did not waste time. When he needed to do something, he acted. She continued:

> I agreed. When we arrived, my parents were still awake. We entered the home, and my father said, "Who is this young man?" and I replied, "He is a friend of mine." My father asked him where he is from, and Tonga Toutai told him he was from Haʻapai. Then he said, "I've come because I hope that you will allow your daughter to be my wife. I will be returning to Haʻapai to complete my work responsibilities." Then my father asked me, "Hēhea, what do you want to do?"
>
> I was unsure. We did not really know each other. I told my father that I was hesitant. But I did know I should be his spouse, so I agreed. We did not waste any time.
>
> We were married on the following Thursday, January 28, 1949, by Misi Emili (Mission President Emile Dunn) at the very first church (LDS), the Matavaimoʻui branch. That Saturday, we sailed to Haʻapai, and we traveled throughout the islands where Tonga Toutai worked as a teacher (Kinikini "Luʻisa Hēhea Pāletuʻa Interview").

Tonga Toutai records the following about the day they were married:

> We were married in Matavaimoʻui just a few weeks before I was to leave for my new teaching assignment on the island of Matuku. After the ceremony, President

Emile Dunn ordained me to the Melchizedek Priesthood and set Hēhea and me apart as missionaries in every village in Tonga where I might be assigned to teach (Shumway 211).

The Kona'ī family. Left to right: Selu, (child), Tangivale, Tēvita, 'Emeline, Esita, Pīliote, Ngatū, Simaima, Hēhea. Taken on the day Esita left for the United States.

Hēhea's family was very different than Tonga Toutai's family. The Kona'ī family were active members of the LDS Church. Her father, Tēvita Kona'ī, had embraced the gospel when he was thirty years old. He married Mosiana Ngatū soon afterward, and they raised all their children in the gospel. The Kona'ī family was humble, warm, and loving. Their lives revolved around the gospel. Hēhea came from a family with ten children: Pīliote, Seluvaia, 'Akesa, Tangivale, 'Emeline, Siale, Luisa Hēhea, Meleseini, 'Ana, and Simaima. There were nine girls and one boy. Hēhea was the seventh child.

There was a profound trust between Tonga Toutai and Hēhea. She said that when she would go to town and spend money, Tonga Toutai would never ask about it. No questions about what she purchased. He trusted her judgment and knew she would always choose what was best for their family. They never argued about money. They spoke kindly to each other and shared a mutual love and respect (Kinikini "Hēhea Lu'isa Pāletu'a Interview").

'Akesiu shared her experience of watching her mother's support of Tonga Toutai with all of his responsibilities. She shared the following:

> Hēhea was not a woman of many words. She worked. She showed her love through her actions. She would wake up early and prepare food for him, and when he returned in the evenings, she would be there to share food and sit with him at the table and talk. She loved him, and he loved her, and they took care of each other (Vaisa "'Akesiu Vainuku Interview").

Their different personalities supported each other. One of Tonga Toutai's strengths was doing what was right; acting immediately regardless of the consequences. He was bold. He cared if people were doing things incorrectly and correct them if necessary. As a missionary, he felt a desire to help all people improve. If someone were doing something wrong, regardless of their status, he would correct them.

One of Hēhea's strengths was in her charity and compassion towards all people. She was warm, welcoming, and friendly. She was personable and attuned to the needs of those around her.

Tonga Toutai and Hēhea had different but complementary roles in their service. They each worked independently but complimentary of each other in every calling. The strength of their relationship was necessary as the years progressed, and their responsibilities in church service grew.

From Makeke to Liahona College

The decision was made to construct a new school, Liahona College. Makeke would be absorbed into the new school, which would provide education to more students on a larger campus. The land was secured for the new school. Makeke would discontinue, and the new school would be built on the new property. Liahona would provide secular and spiritual education to Tongans. The mission records report the following:

> During the year 1949, we have put most of our efforts on the completion of Liahona College. The saints have supported the building program very well. Each branch of the two Tongatapu districts have taken their turn working for a week at a time. The men from Vava'u and Ha'apai and Niuatoputapu have come and stayed a month or more at a time. Twelve or more men have worked and stayed here at Liahona continuously. The schoolboys have worked a week at a time to reach class, and they have provided food for the men who have stayed continually (Pāletu'a, diary).

When he was available, Tonga Toutai would help in the building of the school. They continued to fulfill Tonga's assignments with the government as an educator to various locations throughout the kingdom.

Hēhea shared the following about their life during this time:

> Everywhere we traveled, we helped establish the church: Matuku, Mo'unga'one, and today, there are chapels in each of these areas. We returned to Tongatapu and continued our work with the Church (Kinikini "Hēhea Lu'isa Pāletu'a Interview").

Tonga Toutai and Hēhea.

Tonga Toutai echoed the same sentiments:

> My service as a primary school headteacher for the Tongan Department of Education allowed me to preach the full gospel of Jesus Christ in many villages and islands in the Kingdom of Tonga: Hā'ano, Mo'unga'one, Hōfoa, Fāhefa, Talafo'ou, Nomuka, Faleloa, and Fatai. In each of these places, I was able to nourish friendships and plant the seeds of faith in hundreds of people (Shumway 211).

Pictures 1923 - 1950

L.D.S. Congregations, like this picture of members in Matavaimo'ui in 1937, developed strong community ties. It was the community of members like this that Tonga Toutai was welcomed and embraced while attending school in Nuku'alofa.

Ermel Morton was a young missionary who was assigned the difficult task of translating the Book or Mormon into Tongan. He served his mission in Tonga from 1936-1939. The Book of Mormon was translated during the time Tonga Toutai was learning about the Church. The Book of Mormon would be published in Tongan in April 1946.

Travel around the islands during this time depended on boats. The reliability of transportation was determined by the availability of a boat already going where you needed to go, space, weather and payment.

The Makeke School was created by mission president Vernon Coombs to educate, teach and as a proselyting tool. This school would expand, move locations and become Liahona College.

Queen Sālote was still a teenager when she became the ruler of Tonga. In an effort to maintain her crown decisions were made to protect her status. One such act was the Paassport Act which forbid any future missionaries from entering Tonga. The relationship between the monarchy and the church would improve over the years.

This 5,300 ton vessel, the Tofua, came to Tonga once a month with supplies. Visits to Tonga were infrequent and difficult to secure during the 1920's-1931

Pictures 1923 - 1950

Mission President Evon Huntsman gives Queen Sālote a copy of the Book of Mormon in 1947. This is one of the first copies of the Book of Mormon as it was printed in April 1946. Relationships would continue to improve between the church and the monarchy.

Tonga Toutai worked to pay his way through school including work as a house boy.

The work as a houseboy would include doing chores, labor around the home, running errands as needed.

Lu'isa Hēhea Kona'ī first met Tonga Toutai in Ha'apai when she was visiting her brother, Pīliote, who was serving a mission. They would meet later in Tongatapu at a dance and Tonga would propose to her the same night. She agreed and they were married and (at the same time) set apart as missionaries. They began their marriage establishing the church wherever they traveled. Their missionary service would last their entire lives. Tonga Toutai and Hēhea were fiercely devoted to each other. Tonga Toutai's story is incomplete without Hēhea. She brought out the best in him. Their commitment to God and each other sustained them through difficult and challenging times.

Chapter 3

Forward With Faith | 1950-1959

Search diligently, pray always, and be believing, and all things shall work together for your good.
Doctrine and Covenants 90:24

War Ends, Tonga is Noticed and Church Growth

The Second World War was over, and countries were rebuilding. The kingdom of Tonga had experienced westernization for a time during the war, and soon, the acquisition of material wealth introduced new cultural challenges. As the western world was making an impact in Tonga, the world would also learn more about the graciousness of Tongans.

The Kingdom of Tonga was still under British protection, and matters of Great Britain were of great interest to Tongans. In 1953, Queen Sālote attended the coronation of Queen Elizabeth II. After the coronation ceremonies, as her carriage was traveling through the streets of London in the rain, she requested the hood remain up so she could celebrate with the people who were standing on both sides of the road. She waved and celebrated with the people in the rain. That gesture endeared her and the Kingdom of Tonga, to the world. Queen Sālote invited Queen Elizabeth II to visit Tonga, and she accepted. The Queen of England visited Tonga in December of that same year.

Meanwhile, the steady growth in church membership worldwide would require the need for more temples. The church reached a milestone in 1947 with one million members, and the numbers were still growing by 1950. Of those one million members, 2,820 were from the small island Kingdom of Tonga ("Tonga" 1:3:24). The new decade would initiate the construction of the first temples outside of the continental

United States in Bern, Switzerland, London, England, and Auckland, New Zealand. The South Pacific, for all its remoteness, would now have two temples in its region.

Family Life Begins

On February 11, 1950, Tonga Toutai and Hēhea welcomed their first child, a girl. Traditional Tongan custom allows someone other than the parents to name a child. The naming of a child determined by someone of a higher social rank on the paternal side of the family. However, in this case, it was through Tonga Toutai's maternal side. Tonga Toutai's first cousin, Tu'ipulotu was attending school in New Zealand and named the baby, Tangiteina Lesieli.

Tonga Toutai's employment with the government education program required him to travel and work in different villages. At the time their first child was born, Hēhea returned to her parent's home in Matahau on the main island of Tongatapu. She cared for the new baby with the help of her family for a few weeks before rejoining her husband on his rotation. He was working in Ha'ano as the headmaster of the school during this time.

Tonga Toutai continued to share the gospel as he worked and traveled. On December 10, 1950, he confirmed Penisini 'Ukamea in Fua'motu, Tongatapu.

The family was then assigned to work in Mo'ungaone, the home village of Viliami Pāletu'a, Tonga Toutai's father. The Pāletu'a family were nobles. It was during this time that they welcomed their second and final child, on November 19, 1951. She was given the name, Salome 'Akesiu Mei Hakau Pāletu'a by Matila 'Anau. Tonga Toutai blessed her (Mapa 4).

Classes Begin at Liahona College

The task of building the school fell on the Tongan members of the church and contractors from outside of Tonga to guide the process along. On February 11, 1952, the Liahona College started classes, although the campus was not finished.

The staff consisted of several Tongan teachers and five foreign teaching missionaries. The building was still under construction at this time, but the school was open. Concerns about the "Mormons" continued

Matthew Cowley laying the cornerstone for Liahona College. 1948. (Morton Collection)

from the government, so a legal prohibition forbidding teachers at Liahona from proselyting was put in place.

This ban, however, did not apply to Tonga Toutai and Hēhea who were educators for the government. They would continue their work and proselyte in every village they were assigned. While the government was silencing efforts at the school, Tonga Toutai was still sharing the gospel as a teacher.

During 1952 they would spend the first part of the school year managing the school at Hofoa, and then they transferred to Fahefa for the latter part of the year. He stayed active in his church callings and sharing the gospel. Tonga Toutai's record states that on July 6, 1952, he baptized 'Onetaka Nanumaki Latai.

Tonga Toutai also volunteered time to build Liahona College. In building the college, Tonga Toutai recalled that he became an "expert at shoveling sand." Building missionaries, at the time, would work volunteer hours during the day and then proselyte in the evening. It was a busy schedule.

Liahona College

Liahona College was ready to open on December 1, 1953. The school was open, and the church sent an Apostle to dedicate the property. Elder LeGrand Richards dedicated the school, and Queen Sālote attended the dedication ceremonies.

The significance of Liahona College cannot be underestimated. It was the fruit from the labor of dedicated missionaries over decades of service in Tonga. Starting originally as Makeke, Liahona college was a sign of permanency. The one-hundred-year lease on the property was an indication that the gospel was in Tonga to stay, despite previous efforts to thwart missionary work. Liahona College would educate Tongans in things both temporal and spiritual.

One of the best accounts from the dedication of Liahona can be found in Evon W. Huntsman's written history. He served as Mission President of the Tonga Mission from 1946-1948. He returned to Tonga for the dedication of the school with Elder LeGrand Richards.

The following is taken directly from his written history.

> I was called by the First Presidency, to accompany Apostle LeGrand Richards to Tonga, to dedicate the Liahona College. This was a most wonderful experience, traveling nearly six weeks in constant association with Elder Richards (Huntsman 2002).

Brother Huntsman's experience with Elder Richards shows how difficult it was to make a trip to Tonga. They traveled by plane, bus, mail airplane and boats. He continues:

> We landed at a small Airport near Suva (Fiji) and went by Taxi to the Grand Pacific Hotel. The next morning, we boarded the Matua for Nuku'alofa, Tonga, a thirty-six-hour trip, some 800 miles.

Arriving in Tongatapu was a treat for Brother Huntsman.

> As we entered the harbor, my fourth time and Elder Richards first, it was most beautiful, just between daybreak and sun up. Elder Richards told the Saints, later in Conference, that he now knew I loved them very much, as he was afraid, I would jump overboard and swim to shore before they got the boat tied up and the gangplank down. I will admit, it was a great thrill to meet President and Sister Coombs, the Elders and Saints and friends.

Brother Huntsman shared his excitement of seeing the fruits of his work become a reality.

> One of the great thrills of my life was when we were taken out to Liahona Plantation. As we got out of the car, at the front gate and started to walk up the wide path, with the students lined up on both sides, the band I tried for some time to get organized before we were released, played, "We Thank Thee O God For A Prophet" in honor of Apostle Richards and then burst forth with the

Elder LeGrand Richards and Evon Huntsman.

Tongan National Anthem. We were royally welcomed and entertained by all, with programs and big feasts. The next day was conference. The big auditorium was filled with Queen Sālote, Prince Tuipelehake, many other chieftains, President and Sister Coombs, Officials of the Tongan Government, Rev. McKay of the Tongan State Church, Elders, Lady Missionaries, District and Branch Officers filling the stage. Elder Lindsay and the College Choir sat immediately in front of the pulpit. President and Sister Coombs, myself, Queen Sālote and Apostle Richards spoke, then President Richards dedicated the college for the uplifting and blessings of the Saints. What a thrill to me. The Saints had worked so hard and had made plans for a grand welcome, in the Tongan custom, in place of the afternoon session of Conference. Elder Richards asked me some questions about it. Of course, this was all new to him and somewhat of a change from the Conference held in Zion. I said, "Elder Richards, it will break their hearts if you refuse their request." He said, "We won't do that. "When President Coombs told them, at the close of the session, they could proceed with their feast and *katoanga*; they were a happy people. Mats and braided polos soon began to appear. We walked around the buildings and grounds and went to the Principal's home, Elder and Sister Morton, where we were treated with cocoa, fruit, and cookies. This was called an English Tea, only it was Mormon Cocoa to us, but the Europeans, the Queen, and others enjoyed it.

We were called back to the school about 2:00 pm, to

the feed, as we call them and what a sight, especially for Elder Richards. There were tons of food - baked pork, fish, beef, yams, sweet potatoes, taro, and fruits of all kinds. The afternoon was spent in native songs, dances, speeches, presentation of gifts to Elder Richards, Queen Sālote, and myself. Then a dance at night and we were taken back to the Mission Home for our second nights rest. After breakfast and much visiting with the Elders, and Saints, the Sea Plane came in about noon and we went to the wharf, where we said "*Nofoa*" or goodbye, to hundreds who had gathered from various branches and school children, got in a small launch and were taken out to the plane, anchored about 1/4 mile out and in a few minutes we were off for Fiji, leaving Tonga once more, with a heavy heart, wet eyes full of appreciation for the blessing that had been mine to see Liahona started, built and dedicated (Huntsman).

Liahona College was open. Members of the Church could now receive faith-based education.

Working and Serving

At the time of Liahona's beginnings, Tonga Toutai was still working for the Tonga Department of Education, teaching and managing schools throughout the islands. Working for the government provided Tonga Toutai and Hēhea with a steady income. Not only were they being paid by the government, they would also receive donations and gifts (such as food and tapacloth) or other offerings from the families of the children Tonga Toutai taught (Kinikini "Hēhea Interview").

While employed with the government, he also served in branches wherever they lived. In 1954, Tonga Toutai was serving as second counselor in the Ha'akame Branch Presidency. He was released on February 28, 1955. He would then be called to serve as second counselor of the Hihifo District Sunday School Presidency on August 27, 1955.

Leaving Government Work for Liahona College

After Liahona College opened, Tonga Toutai was asked to fill a teaching position at the new church school. The culmination of culture, religion, and education had prepared him to fulfill this new responsibility. His record states the following:

> In January 1955, I received a new calling from the Mission President, D'Monte Coombs, and Elder J. Morton, Principal of Liahona, if I would be a teacher at Liahona. So, we moved to Liahona. I started work as an assistant to Brother Patrick D. Dalton. We worked with the Cowboys in the farm. (1974, Mapa)
>
> It was a labor of love. When I notified the Department of Education of my intentions, the reply came: "If you leave your position and move to Liahona, that's the end of your service with the DOE."
>
> I was pleased to go and be part of this exciting educational venture in Liahona. Thus began a long association with students and leaders (Shumway 212)

The decision to move from a stable, government job to work at the new church school was an uncertain gamble. The school was a new enterprise. There were governmental pressures to keep teachers from proselyting. He would move from being in charge of running schools to a faculty member. If the school, for whatever reason, failed, he would no longer be able to teach. Despite these considerations, he and Hēhea chose to accept the call.

On February 7, 1955, Tonga Toutai began working at Liahona college. He was one of a growing number of native Tongan teachers. It opened that year with 237 students. The faculty members of Liahona College included:

Elder Ermel Morton: Principal
Sister Morton: Bookstore, Bookkeeping, Sewing
Brother Bulkley: Agriculture, Nature Study
Sister Buckley: Hygiene, Animal Husbandry, Drawing
Sister Dalton: Typewriting, Shorthand, Reading, Office Work
Elder Lindsay: English, Sports
Elder Peck: Reading, Band, Music
Elder Graham: English
Sovea Kioa: Arithmetic
Atonio Tu'iasoa: Tongan, Music, Tongan Crafts
Semisi Nukumovaha'i Tonga: Arithmetic, Tongan crafts, Nature study
Tonga Toutai Pāletu'a: Tongan Language, Hygiene, Arithmetic
Sione Tuita: History, Geography
Semisi Taumoepeau: Carpentry, Tongan crafts, Tongan language

Filimone Fie'eiki: Office assistant, Bookkeeping, Hygiene
Fa'alupenga Sanft: Sewing, Cookery (also in charge of the girls)
Tu'iasoa in charge of boys generally
Fakatou Vaitai: Mechanics, Mechanical Repairs
Sione Taufa: Garden Assistant

During this time, they attended the Liahona Branch, where they served in various callings. They were called to serve as teachers in the Mutual. Tonga Toutai also held responsibilities as a Sunday School teacher and a Quorum President. Later this year, during a leadership meeting, Tonga Toutai was set apart as a building missionary, although he was already volunteering to help with the building of the school.

President David O. McKay Visits Tonga

President David O. McKay and his wife Emma Ray visited Tonga in 1955. They were welcomed like royalty. This was the first visit of a Church President to the islands.

During his visit, President McKay revealed that he had seen a vision of "a temple on one of these islands, where members of the Church may go and receive the blessings of the temple of God." These words were shocking. One member recorded the Tongan's response as: "The entire congregation burst into tears." At the time, there were only eight operating temples in the world, most of them in Utah. The idea that a Temple would be built in Tonga seemed impossible, especially considering the remoteness of the islands. There were many reasons to doubt this prophecy, but a seed had been planted in the hearts of Tongan saints. Less than thirty years later, President David O. McKay's words would be fulfilled.

Scouting in Tonga

In 1913 the church officially joined the Boy Scouts of America as its first charter organization, adopting the program as the activity arm of its Mutual Improvement Association. It is no surprise then that missionaries from the United States would carry their love of scouting wherever they served.

Scouting in the Kingdom of Tonga began on June 1, 1935, when Elder Floyd C. Fletcher, a new missionary, received the assignment to introduce the scouting program at Makeke. Twenty years later, the scouting program was still being implemented as part of the church's curriculum.

Scouting appealed to Tonga Toutai. The tenets of scouting to be trustworthy and self-reliant were values Tonga Toutai already embraced. Joining other like-minded Tongans promoting these values would be vital to him.

A week-long scouting conference was held at Liahona College in December 1955. It was conducted by Elder James Christiansen, Mission Scout Director, and Semisi Motulalo Tonga, Assistant Scout Director. The scouts camped at Liahona and ate all of their meals together during the week.

On December 5, 1955, at 6:30 pm, a meeting was held in the auditorium of Liahona College to orient the scouts and explain the week's activity. The agenda for the week included flag raising and lowering ceremonies each day with training sessions throughout the day. Among the skills taught were: First Aid, nature recognition, ax throwing, fire building, singing, knot tying, trestle building, etc. They held contests and enjoyed games. There were over 300 people in attendance during the campfire meetings.

The mission records report the following about the event:

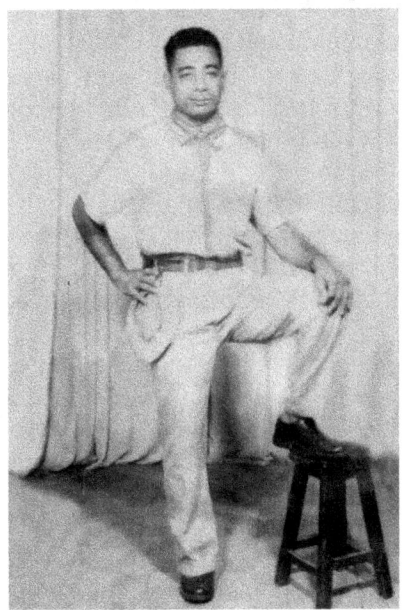

Tonga Toutai in his scouting uniform. (Kinikini Collection)

For all the contests and sports, the scouts were divided up into four patrols during the week: Red patrol, Flying Fox patrol, Owl patrol, and Seagull patrol. Each day one of the patrols were on duty and took care of the daily chores and work. All in all, a very successful training period was carried out, and as it was the first of its kind in the mission, it should add to the scout work in the ensuing years. Thirty scouts and scout leaders participated in the week-long events ("Tonga" 1:3:312-313).

Tonga Toutai participated in this scout training in preparation for an event at the end of the December. The following is recorded in Allan E. Morton's Chronology:

> December 22, 1955 - The Buckleys leave Tonga for America on an airplane. Also, leaving today is Tonga Toutai Pāletu'a. He was a Liahona teacher going to Australia for a Boy Scout meeting.
> Only four Tongans made the trip: Sinisa Fakalata, Senituli Manu, 'Unga Ma'afu Tupou, and himself (Mapa 5).

They represented the Kingdom of Tonga and the Church in Australia at the 5th Pan Pacific Jamboree. The Jamboree was held a Clifford Park, Victoria. Over 16,000 scouts from over 20 countries attended the event. The Jamboree officially opened on December 30, 1955, and officially closed on January 8, 1956.

This would have been Tonga Toutai's first time outside of the Kingdom of Tonga.

Honesty, At All Cost

The decision was made to live in Liahona and work at the school indefinitely. Tonga Toutai and Hēhea decided the build a home close to the school rather than living on campus. Because he had helped to build Liahona College, he was skilled at building this new home. He would, throughout his life, build another home by himself.

An experience he had while building this house taught his daughter, Tangiteina, a valuable lesson. Tangiteina remembers going with her father to Nuku'alofa to pick up lumber and other supplies needed to build their house. On the drive, she remembers her father was anxious to get the materials to begin working.

When they arrived to purchase the materials to build the home, she saw her father leave the truck and talk to another man. They loaded the materials he asked for, and she noticed her father and the man were still talking. The communication seemed to go on for a long time, and then she saw her father giving the other man money. The man refused and tried to give it back to Tonga Toutai, but Tonga Toutai was insistent. The man accepted, shaking his head. Tonga Toutai got back into the car.

Tangiteina asked her father what happened, and her father told her that the man, his friend, told him to take the materials without paying. His friend promised that no one would ever know. He said the man offered them as a gift and as an act of friendship. The gesture was

Tonga and Hehea with their children Tangiteina and 'Akesiu at Liahona.

out of kindness. The tradition of giving something for free is common among Tongans.

As a young father, supporting his family, the offer would have been tempting. He could save money and perhaps use it elsewhere, even in the name of building the kingdom in other ways. The family was already saving money to pay for a trip to the New Zealand Temple to be sealed. Perhaps the offer was a gift from Heavenly Father to help them reach that goal.

Tonga Toutai knew better.

He told his daughter he could not accept the offer. "How can I say a prayer to Heavenly Father and know that the roof of my house was built by dishonesty?"

Tonga Toutai taught his daughter two profound lessons that day: first, dishonesty is never acceptable no matter how it is justified, and second, Tonga Toutai's relationship to Heavenly Father was more important to him than anything else (Kinikini "Tangiteina Interview").

Tonga Toutai and Hēhea built their home across the street from Liahona.

Back to Family

Tonga Toutai and Hēhea's new life as a family in Liahona seemed complete, and yet, the years had not changed his love for his parents and family. As was his nature, Tonga Toutai spoke to them about the need to be baptized and to join the church, but they refused.

Viliami visited his son, Tonga Toutai, at Liahona College. Tangiteina remembers meeting her grandfather in Liahona and that they took a picture together. She recalls that he was "a big man. He was very tall." Tonga Toutai, Hēhea, and the children also visited Viliami and Milika Mafi in Pangai. Tangiteina remembers feeling loved by her grandmother, but it was the last time they met (Kinikini, "Tangiteina Interview").

Viliami remained a faithful minister in his church, and Tonga Toutai remained committed to following his faith in the Church of Jesus Christ of Latter-day Saints.

New Zealand Temple to be Sealed

The goal of every Tongan member of the church was to receive the ordinances of the temple, but there were many obstacles. The closest temple to Tonga was in Hamilton, New Zealand. The cost of travel prohibited many families from making the trip. Many saved money for years to attend. Some families, like the Viliami and Luisa Kongaika family, sold every material possession they had to pay for the trip, with no thought of where they would live when they returned to Tonga. Tonga Toutai and Hēhea were determined to sacrifice whatever was needed to be sealed in the temple. After carefully managing their finances, they had saved enough to make the trip. They planned to go with a small group of Tongan families in December of 1958. This was the second group of Tongans saints to make such a trip.

The Pāletu'a family arrived in New Zealand and were sealed as a family on December 31, 1958. They remained in New Zealand for a few weeks to attend the temple. During this time, they performed work for their Tongan ancestors, and among them was Tonga Toutai's brother, Sione Masalu, who had passed away suddenly at the age of seventeen when Tonga Toutai was thirteen years old.

Chapter 4

Preparing the Way | 1960 - 1969

Be thou humble; and the Lord thy God shall lead thee by the hand, and give thee answer to thy prayers.
Doctrine and Covenants 112:10

Queen Sālote passes away

The decade of the 1960s would see changes in the monarchy. Beloved Queen Sālote would pass away in 1965 after ruling the kingdom for 47 years, three months, and 25 days.

At the beginning of her reign, she supported legislation against the growth of missionary work in Tonga. The denial of visas for missionaries hindered the work initially. She also refused to see visiting missionaries in the palace; however, over time, she became a friend, as evidenced by her participation in the dedication ceremonies of Liahona High School and in accepting a Book of Mormon from Mission President Evon W. Huntsman in 1947.

Queen Sālote's reign and opinion of the L.D.S. Church in Tonga is almost representative of Tongans and their relationship with the restored gospel during the same period of time. It was difficult for many to accept the gospel at first; however, over time, there was more than just acceptance; there was appreciation.

After Queen Sālote's death, the mourning period of six months began for every Tongan citizen. Tongan custom forbids dancing, loud singing, loud music, and sports. Black clothing and mourning mats were prepared. Female members of the family either cut their hair or wore it unkempt. Weeding gardens was prohibited during the mourning period. On the nights of December 20-22, the ceremony of *takipō* was observed: groups of people sat just beyond the Palace walls, each group burning a torch over clean sand. The flames would be cared for throughout the night (Wood-Ellem 289-290).

Queen Sālote's son, Taufa'ahau Tupou IV, would take her place. He had previously encouraged the building of Liahona. New relationships between the church and Tonga were forming that would increase the success of the gospel work throughout the kingdom. His coronation took place on July 4, 1967. Mission President John H. Groberg and his wife Jean were invited to attend.

Liahona, Radio, and Miracles

Liahona High School was a bustling school with activities, events, and its own issues. The school held performances for visiting tourists to the islands. These visitors were often impressed with the Liahona campus because of its modernity. The community in Liahona also housed a large number of *pāpalangi* families with children. There were births, deaths, marriages. Foreign and native teachers were coming and going constantly. Students came from Tonga, Tahiti, and Fiji. One year there was a strike where the young men walked out of Liahona High School and went to the beach. They protested against some of the staff and demanded changes. The faculty unsuccessfully tried to get the male students to return to the school. Eventually, the boys and school administration agreed to meet to discuss the issue the next morning. When the boys arrived in the morning, they each received a letter telling them they were expelled from school. If they wanted to return, they would have to come with a parent (and those from other islands would have Brother Patrick Dalton as a parent representative) to be readmitted. Tonga Toutai was put in charge of the interviews for readmittance (Nixon, journal). Liahona was a bustling, active community that provided Tonga Toutai with first-hand experience with how the church works and how to problem-solve issues with people.

In 1961, Tonga Toutai and Hēhea took on responsibilities over the boys' dormitory as house parents at Liahona College. They would care for and monitor the young men. There were strict rules in Liahona that forbid boys and girls from dating. The school wanted students to focus on education.

Some of Tonga Toutai's responsibilities at Liahona included recruiting and admissions. On September 16, 1966, he traveled with Aaron Christensen (another teacher) to Vava'u and Ha'apai to test prospective students for school entrance. These trips would take around two weeks to complete.

Life in Liahona was an opportunity to meet and get acquainted with people from around the world. Tonga Toutai mingled with Bob White, a teacher who was driving in Nuku'alofa when his car hit a Tongan man. Tonga Toutai was a passenger and reported to the police that the man was dressed in black and could not be seen from the road. The Tongan who was hit also did not blame Brother White for the accident.

Tonga Toutai also had opportunities to preach in meetings. It was said that he was more soft-spoken in his delivery of speeches than his Tongan counterparts who would preach in the Tongan *faifekau* style (Nixon, journal).

Additional responsibilities seemed to come to Tonga Toutai and Hēhea during this time. Tonga Toutai preached on the radio station providing weekly sermons on the radio. The gospel was now being shared through the airwaves throughout the Kingdom of Tonga. He offered these weekly radio sermons from 1961 until 1968. He continued to preach sermons on the radio throughout his life. In addition to his teaching duties, Tonga Toutai also began to serve as the chief correction officer at Liahona High School. In 1963 he was called as an assistant to President Dalton in the Tonga Nuku'alofa Mission.

Tonga Toutai was able to see miracles during his work. The following is an experience he shared in *Tongan Saints: Legacy of Faith*:

> I remember a conference in Vava'u, which I attended with mission president Patrick Dalton when we were invited to the village of Koloa for a meal. A severe drought had scourged the land for a long time, and water was very scarce. As we sat down to the dinner, the branch president leaned over to President Dalton and said, "There is something I would like to ask the person who prays. We desperately need rain. There is no water in the land."
>
> Of course, this was long before community water pumps came into being. President Dalton looked searchingly around at the crowd. Finally, he said, "Tonga Toutai, stand and pray for us, and ask the Lord to send rain."
>
> The noonday sun was beating down hard on the congregation. I was given an order to bring rain, to open the doors of heaven and bless all of Vava'u, the land, and the people. After my fervent prayer, I sat down to the meal. Suddenly (and very obviously) clouds began to gather over the land, lightly shading us at first, then transforming themselves into a thick dark covering. The meal had

not finished when the first drops of rain in many months began to fall. By the end of the meal, everything was wet. When we went back to our meetings in Ha'alaufuli, the rain was still falling. This moisture was the greatest blessing of the conference. It was not just my faith, but the power of the command of authority for me to pray that made the difference (Shumway 212-213).

More opportunities to serve began to emerge for Tonga Toutai and Hēhea. In 1964, he was called as Assistant to the District President under Pres. Buckley. The following year he was called as the District President over the Hihifo area of Tonga. Hēhea was by his side supporting and helping fulfill these responsibilities.

These callings and the associations he made with other church members shaped his leadership style. He shared the following:

> As I think of the great men who groomed and prepared me for my many responsibilities in the church, I realize my heavy debt to them all. From Sovea Kioa, I learned skill and poise, both in public and in personal relations and especially in ceremonial settings with royalty and the nobility. From Misitana Vea, I learned serenity, how a great leader should love his wife and family, and how to rebuke the Saints with love. From President Emile Dunn, I learned the value of consistent hard work and straight talk to the members. He understood and loved Tongans as well as anyone (212).

Tonga Toutai's records are filled with the names of people he associated with throughout his life and are often accompanied by brief descriptions of how they are connected. Many of them were influential to his development as a person, and he documented their names. While becoming a teacher, he recognized the need to keep learning, and he absorbed the goodness of those around him.

Formation of the Hihifo District

On July 10, 1966, the Liahona District was dissolved and combined with the Hihifo District. Tonga Toutai was called as the district president with Bert Nixon as first counselor and Aliki Vimahi as second counselor. During the blessings to set apart this presidency, Mission President John H. Groberg stated that "a stake would be organized in Tonga in a short time." It seemed impossible.

Mission Presidency with President Groberg

In 1966, John H. Groberg was called to serve as the Mission President replacing President Patrick Dalton. On August 2, Manase Nau was called as the first counselor, and Tonga Toutai was called as the second counselor. Tonga Toutai was prepared to fulfill this calling because he had accepted previous assignments and callings and served with faithfulness.

It was a busy time for missionary work in Tonga. Tonga Toutai would continue his work at Liahona High School as a teacher to support his family as well as serve the needs of the mission. President Groberg would encourage and prove the faith of Tongan saints in unique ways during his tenure as mission president. President Groberg was equal parts bold and loving. He expected a lot from the Tongans, and they proved they could meet those expectations. President Groberg also had a strong relationship with the royal family.

Everyone goes through personal struggles. In 1967, Tonga Toutai and Hēhea were about to face a family situation that would challenge Tonga Toutai's belief in himself and possibly derail his confidence as a leader of the church in Tonga.

How Can I Serve When My Family is Falling Apart?

Amid the growth of the church and the increasing responsibilities Tonga Toutai and Hēhea were facing, they were also raising two children. Their children were both teenagers. He had raised them in a respectable home. The family, by nature of their service, were considered examples and pillars of their community. On the surface, they were a perfect family. Tonga Toutai was a leader supported by his devoted wife and two daughters attending Liahona High School.

While at school, Tangiteina, their eldest daughter, met a young man by the name of Pita Kinikini. He had come from 'Uiha. She said she first met Pita in class when he asked her for a pencil. Tangiteina said, "No." and walked away. Inspired or excited by her disinterest in him, he continued to stare at her during the remainder of the class. That prompted Tangiteina to turn away in frustration.

He began sending messages through his friends to Tangiteina's friends. Tangiteina was not impressed and rejected his advances.

Tangiteina worked in the bookstore, and Pita would frequently come to the bookstore to try and speak to her. Tangiteina reported she would hide in the back or tell him to go away, but he persisted. He was

Mission President Groberg with Tonga Toutai. 1968. (Kinikini Collection)

interested in her. The interest continued but in discreet ways. During a student talent show at Liahona High School, Pita sang a song and had told his classmates that it was dedicated to Tangiteina. She was not amused, and yet his persistence was endearing. He did not give up. Something was calming about his presence.

As their friendship blossomed, they had to keep it private. Liahona High School had a very strict policy that forbids dating or students pairing off as a couple on school property.

One evening a teacher saw Pita talking to Tangiteina by the fence of the school. He reported it to administration, and the following day Pita was expelled.

Despite being expelled, Pita did not disappear. He was still performing in his band, the "Liahona 7" around the island, and also for school dances. Pita also attended school dances when he could. With the help of their friends, someone would ask Tangiteina and lead her to the center of the gymnasium. Pita's friends would smuggle him into the middle to meet her while friends acted as a shield from faculty. Some faculty encouraged the relationship. Tangiteina's typing teacher would tell her where Pita was practicing with his band and excuse her to see him.

The majority of Pita's family emigrated to the United States, and Pita's father, Tēvita Muli Kinikini, sent word to have Pita come to Hawaii. Pita was leaving Tonga, probably permanently. The idea of leaving Tangiteina was difficult for him, so he proposed marriage.

The time was short. They agreed to get married during school, in secret, with the help of Pita's older brother, Senituli. On September 24, 1967, Tangiteina dressed and went to school like she had done so many mornings before. When she arrived at the school, Senituli was waiting at the front entrance with a taxi. She entered the taxi, hid her head, and they drove to Nuku'alofa to meet Pita. They were able to get a license from the government to be married, but they still needed someone to marry them.

They rushed to find someone to officiate the ceremony. They found Tupou Malekamu, a President of the Vaini Branch.

The minister seemed to recognize Tangiteina and asked, "What is your name? Who are your parents?"

Tangiteina replied, "My name is Tangiteina Pāletu'a."

The minister then shook his head and said, "I will not marry you. I know your father. You go home."

Things were not going to go as planned. Pita's brother, Senituli, encouraged President Malekamu to perform the marriage, and so he did, reluctantly. They were officially husband and wife.

Eventually, Tonga Toutai and Hēhea heard about Tangiteina "running away" to get married. They were shocked. They immediately drove around the island, looking for their daughter. They went with Aliki, Tonga Toutai's cousin. The goal was to find Tangiteina and bring her home. They found her with Pita's family.

Tonga Toutai and Hēhea said their daughter was too young to be married and told her to return home with them. Aliki intervened and asked Tangiteina what she wanted to do. Tangiteina said she wanted to stay with Pita. It was with a heavy heart that Tonga Toutai and Hēhea returned home without their daughter.

The next day, Tonga Toutai met with President Groberg. He asked for an immediate release from his calling as a counselor in the Mission Presidency. Elder Groberg related the following in an interview:

> He came in and told me he needed to be released from his calling. He told me he could not teach the people because his daughter ran away and got married. He said it would be embarrassing for the church. I told him, "No. You will not be released." I told him everything would be okay and that the Lord has a plan for Teina and Pita, but the Lord needed him to serve. He was emotional and cried. He kept insisting, but I told him everything would be okay (Kinikini, "Groberg Interview").

Tonga Toutai agreed to remain as a counselor in the mission presidency. The cultural shame Tonga Toutai felt was challenged by the counsel he received from President Groberg. He knew President Groberg was called of God.

Culturally, Tongans believe church leaders possess a certain *mana* (spiritual power) that protects them and their children from worldly problems. President Groberg taught Tonga Toutai that everyone, even leaders of the church, face challenges. He also taught Tonga Toutai that leaders of the church are not perfect. It was a powerful lesson he would carry for the rest of his life.

There were murmurings among the Tongan saints, but instead of ignoring it, he addressed it. Members of the church reported to Tangiteina that during Tonga Toutai's sermons, he would chastise parents to teach their young men not to "steal" young women. The reference was clear. Still, he trusted President Groberg's counsel and was buoyed by his encouragement. He worked hard to fulfill his calling.

A New Stake in Tonga

In April 1968, Elder Thomas S. Monson visited the Tonga mission and concluded that Tonga was ready for a stake. There were enough members, priesthood leadership, and experience in Tonga. Upon returning to Salt Lake City, Elder Monson recommended to the Twelve Apostles that the first stake should be created. President Groberg received notice on June 16 from Salt Lake City that the stake would be organized.

Elder Thomas S. Monson and Elder Howard W. Hunter arrived in Tonga on September 4 to organize the first stake in Tonga. They were greeted at the airport by a large group of saints and the Liahona band. There was excitement among the members.

Elders Hunter and Monson began to interview priesthood leaders to determine who should be the stake president. Elder Monson reported the following about the experience:

> I shall never forget the night we interviewed all of the priesthood brethren that we might organize the very first stake in Tonga. Howard W. Hunter and I were there with our wives. And as we interviewed, everyone would say, "Elder Groberg." and I would say, "No, no, no." and it took a little while to convince them (the saints) that he could not be the mission president and the stake president.

The leadership of the first stake in Tonga. President Orson White with counselors Tonga Toutai Pāletu'a and 'Uliti 'Uata. 1968. (Kinikini Collection)

I recall that our school leader became our stake president, Orson White and I remember his first counselor was Tonga Toutai Pāletu'a and the second counselor was, 'Uliti 'Uata (S.L. Utah)

Orson H. White was working as the superintendent of Church Schools in Tonga. He was experienced in church administration. He had been in several bishoprics, and he had organizational knowledge of church operations. He would teach Tongan leaders how to operate and run a successful stake. Former mission president Jay A. Cahoon was working at Liahona High School and was called as a patriarch for the Kingdom of Tonga.

Elder Thomas S. Monson ordained Tonga Toutai Pāletu'a to the office of High Priest on September 6, 1968.

The opportunity to work under President Orson White taught Tonga Toutai about the nuances of stake organization, administration, and working with the Tongan people. Tonga Toutai was a student again. He took advantage of this opportunity to learn as much as he could. This period of learning was fortuitous as the church in the Kingdom of Tonga was growing so large a second stake of Zion would soon be necessary.

The Parable of the *Makafeke*

During this visit to Tonga, Thomas S. Monson observed Tonga Toutai teaching a class at Liahona High School. He would reference what he learned throughout his life as a modern parable. Elder Monson would reference Tonga Toutai by name in settings where he spoke with Polynesians. In more formal settings, he would only mention he learned a lesson from a Tongan teacher.

In 1993, President Monson shared the following:

> I remember particularly, however, a lesson that I saw taught by Tonga Toutai Pāletu'a in the school where he was a teacher. He had a large class, and he was teaching them how to honor the truth and how to beware of the evil one. He had made some contraption, out of a stick and a couple of coconuts and some leaves. He called it a *makafeke*. An octopus trap. He said how they would row out in the ocean and dangle the makafeke down in the water. And the octopus, thinking that it was a crab of some kind, would come up to the surface and grab it and not let go. And then the fisherman would lift the makafeke and the octopus into the boat, and there would be food, namely the octopus. And as I heard him telling that lesson, I thought to myself, "Satan dangles *makafeke's* in front of you and in front of me. And if we are like the octopus, and do not think and do not observe and do not have the inspiration of the Lord, we can grab the temptation which is put before us. We lose our salvation and our exaltation because we have not listened to the whisperings of the Holy Spirit. I would like to ask you and challenge you today with the creation of this stake to make certain that we turn away from the *makafeke's* of Lucifer and grasp the iron rod of God. Follow his teachings and obey his commandments. And as Paul said to Timothy, "Be thou an example unto the believers (S.L. Utah).

First Trip to Salt Lake City, Utah

The need for local members to receive instruction from church headquarters was crucial in helping local leaders see a broader vision of the gospel work in their lands. In October of 1968, Tonga Toutai and a few other Tongan church leaders traveled to Salt Lake City to attend General Conference. He states the following in his records:

Chapter 4   47

Artist portrayal of Tonga Toutai teaching the lesson about the maka feke. Used by permission of the artist, Chris Hawkes.

In October of 1968, I attended Church Conference with Bishop Mosese Langi, Bishop Folau Mahu'inga, and Water Lily Wolfgramm. At that time, I met President David O. McKay, and we invited President Tanner for the Golden Year Jubilee of the Church in Tonga (Mapa 3).

This would be the first of many trips Tonga Toutai would make to the church's General Conference in Salt Lake City, Utah. At the time, General Conference was held over three days. It included instruction for church leaders during the weeks leading up to the General Conference as well.

Graduation and a First Grandchild

In 1969, 'Akesiu graduated from Liahona High School. Tonga Toutai and Hēhea knew of the importance of the Temple, so they sent 'Akesiu to New Zealand at this time to receive her endowments. 'Akesiu also served for two years as a missionary in Tonga beginning on November 29, 1969, until December 1, 1971.

While serving as the First Counselor in the stake presidency, Tonga Toutai and Hēhea welcomed their first grandchild, a baby girl. She arrived on July 16 and was born in the Nuku'alofa Hospital. As is Tongan custom, Pita's family named the infant Vika Fatafehi Kinikini.

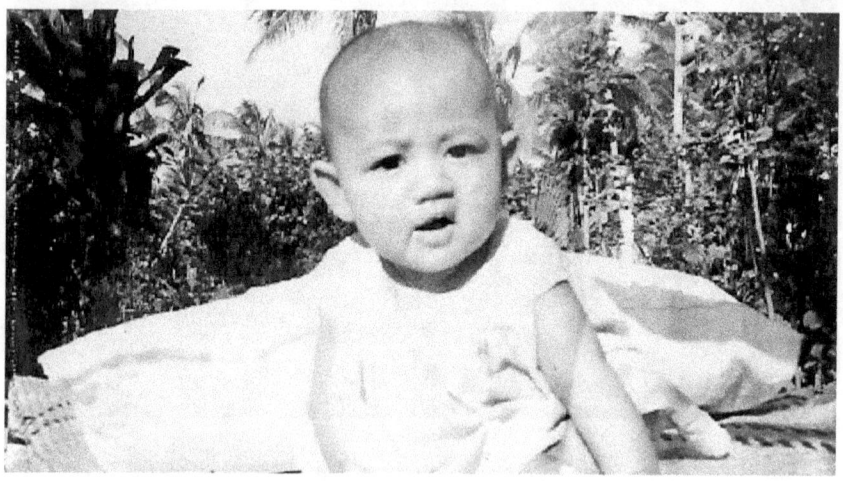

Vika Fatafehi was the first grandchild of Tonga Toutai and Hēhea.

The birth of this grandchild helped to ease relationships. Tangiteina records the following in her journal about the day of the baby blessing:

> 'Auhangamea (Pita's eldest sister) brought a dress and a blanket for the baby. We went to the Latai, Nuku'alofa chapel to bless the baby. She was blessed by John H. Groberg, president of the mission. In the circle stood, Pita, Muli (Pita's father) and Tonga Toutai (Teina, Journal).

Pita and Tangiteina moved back to Liahona and lived with Tonga Toutai and Hēhea so they could help care for the new baby. It was a task that came easily to Hēhea who was loving and devoted to her grandchildren.

Pita began working at Liahona High School (the name had since been changed from Liahona College) driving the bookmobile, a portable library carrying books. Pita also traveled around the island performing in his band for dances and events.

A year later, baby Vika became ill. She was taken to the hospital. The family prayed and fasted for her recovery. President Groberg had a similar experience when his infant son, John Enoch, became ill in Tonga. President Groberg again became a source of comfort and strength as they blessed baby Vika to recover. Vika spent her celebrated her first birthday with the nurses and children in the hospital.

The Church Growth Continues

The formation of the first stake in Tonga came at a busy time for church members. First, the Tonga Mission had 100 baptisms in September, and under the inspiration of President Groberg, he challenged the missionaries to set a goal to baptize 500 new members by the end of the year. Second, the mission was also planning a Golden Jubilee Celebration in November for the first 50 years of the church in Tonga.

The Tongan saints also received a lot of visitors from church headquarters. Bishop Victor L. Brown of the Presiding Bishopric, J. Thomas Fyans, of translation and distribution services, Elder Henry D. Taylor, assistant to the Council of the Twelve and many other visitors came for various training and conferences. President N. Eldon Tanner of the First Presidency sent word that he would attend the Jubilee celebrations in November. He arrived with Lavern Parmley, president of the Primary Association and Kathryn S. Gilbert of the Relief Society General Board.

President Groberg's challenge for baptisms was met. The missionaries had baptized 507 souls just in November. The emphasis of the mission, however, was not on numbers. It was on finding those seeking the truth (Britsch 483).

As missionary work continued throughout Tonga, new chapels were needed. On October 18, 1969, land was blessed for a chapel in Vaotu'u, and on the same day, a parcel of land was blessed in Matangiake to build a chapel and Stake Center. Matangiake is next to Liahona High School. The building in Matangiake would serve as Tonga Toutai and Hēhea's new homeward (Pāletu'a, diary).

Seeking a Christlike Life

Tonga Toutai focused his attention on living a Christlike life. He often prayed throughout the day for spiritual guidance. He frequently fasted. He sought the guidance of the Holy Ghost. As he developed spiritually, he also became more aware of the needs of other people. He sought to serve others in any way he could. He developed a love for all people, and he desired to do what the Savior would do at all times.

Elder John H. Grober shared the following experience he had with Tonga Toutai while visiting neighboring islands.

> Two other leaders from the church and I were visiting a small branch on a distant island in the South Pacific. The island was so small and so remote, as well as having so few members of the church that having three visitors come from America, Europe and Polynesia at the same time was an occasion for great rejoicing.
>
> The outflowing of love and appreciation for our visit was wonderful. The members paid close attention to all that was said, and our meetings were filled with the Spirit. At the conclusion of the meetings, the Saints held a marvelous feast accompanied by superb music and dancing.
>
> As we prepared to leave the next morning, the whole branch came to the wharf to send us on our way. They gave us beautiful leis, lots of hugs, and gifts. The branch president told us that one of the older sisters in the branch had been a pearl diver all her life and had spent weeks diving for our visit. He asked each of us to hold out our hands. Then this older lady carefully placed a small object in each of our outstretched hands.
>
> As I watched the perfectly shaped, exquisitely colored

black pearl slowly roll back and forth in the palm of my hand, it took my breath away. The only thing that shone above the radiance of that beautiful pearl was the light coming from this tiny lady and the joy in the eyes of the branch president and members standing on the beach.

My heart was touched.

How could these Saints, who had so little in terms of worldly possessions, do this for us? Those who needed material things more gave them to others who certainly needed them less, just to show their love and appreciation.

Tears began to well in my eyes, and I wasn't sure what to say. We had simply visited their island, imparted instruction, and born testimony. They, on the other hand, had given more of themselves to us in return. Not only had they expressed their joy and appreciation for our visit and for the renewing of their faith and testimonies, but now they had given these beautiful pearls.

My initial reaction was to give my pearl back and tell them to sell it and use the proceeds for their own temporal needs. However, an inner voice told me to accept the gift humbly and leave the rest to God. He would bless them in the most important ways.

I did my best to express our appreciation for their kindness and assured them that God would bless them for their love and goodness and faithfulness. I concluded with my testimony of the truthfulness of the gospel and the certainty that obedience to God brings great blessings.

I then noticed one leader looking at the pearl in his hand, then at the pearls in the other two hands, concentrating his gaze on the pearl in the hand of the Polynesian leader. Out of curiosity, I looked, and I quickly saw that the pearl in the Polynesian's hand was considerably larger and had a most spectacular glow about it.

As soon as the Polynesian leader sensed what was happening, he instinctively took the pearl from his hand and placed it into the hand of the one who had been staring at it. That man took his smaller pearl and tried to place it into the Polynesian man's hand. However, the Polynesian leader just smiled and said, "No, that's all right. You keep them both. I can get another one if I need it."

I was awestruck. These humble people had given us their best pearls, and now the humble Polynesian leader had instinctively given his to someone else. As I looked at the faithful Polynesian leader, I felt I was in the presence of true greatness. I felt that he had developed that precious Christlike quality of sensing another's needs or desires and then fulfilling them the best he could.

I marveled (and continue to do so) at the magnanimity of such souls. How doe sone become like that? I sensed that this older sister and this Polynesian brother had gotten to the point where they understood that value was not in possessing things, but in showing love and helping others. I was amazed at how instinctively they gave of what they had, and I could see that these actions were a byproduct of who they were. This lady diver gave her best and was happy. This Polynesian leader had no pearl a few minutes earlier; now, just a few minutes later, he still had no pearl, but in the brief interlude, he had traded something of worldly value for something of heavenly value.

I knew this man quite well, but now I had a deeper desire to know him even better. It is one thing to preach the doctrines of Christ; it is quite another to live them. The vain things of the world were not going to canker his soul. The deceitfulness of riches or power or fame were deflected by him, and I could tell he was truly seeking first the kingdom of God. His action brought awe to me, gratitude from his benefactor, peace to himself, and, I'm sure, a smile from God.

Over the next several years I had the opportunity to work with this man on various occasions. Once I gave him a particularly difficult assignment. After explaining it to him, I asked how he felt about accepting it.

As instinctively as he had given his pearl, he responded, "I know the Lord. I trust Him and His servants. I am not afraid to do anything He asks me to do. I know He will help me. So I feel good about accepting this call."

He fulfilled that calling with honor and humility, as he did all callings given to him (Groberg, "Eternity is Now" 77-81).

Calling as a Patriarch

Still, more changes were coming. On November 19, 1969, Tonga Toutai was ordained as a Patriarch for the nation of Tonga by Elder LeGrand Richards. He shares the following in an interview about that experience:

I cannot begin to count my blessings, and it was a top highlight of my whole life. It is a wonderful blessing for me. I was able to give blessings to many of the Saints who came from Vava'u, Ha'apai, Niuafo'ou, Niuatoputapu, 'Eua, Fiji, Tahiti, and including European members (Mapa 6).

Tonga Toutai was the first Tongan to hold the calling of Patriarch. Now, Tongans could receive their Patriarchal blessings in the Tongan language. He performed his first Patriarchal blessings for his daughter, Tangiteina, and son-in-law, Pita.

Family Changes

Pita and Tangiteina were leaving the kingdom of Tonga for the United States. Their decision was based on two factors: first, the majority of Pita's family had already emigrated and were living in Hawaii, and second, Pita was encouraged to go to school. Tonga Toutai, the educator, encouraged the young couple to go; however, they yearned for their two new grandchildren whom they loved. Further encouragement came from Orson White, former Stake President (whom Tonga Toutai served with as First Counselor) and was also the Superintendent of Church Schools in Tonga. He encouraged Pita to go to the United States and then return to serve the people of Tonga.

There was an overwhelming amount of fear. The United States was so foreign to many Tongans at the time. Rumors were circulating about the dangers of living among the *papālangi*. Tangiteina recalled people in Tonga warning them about people stealing children, especially babies. The only connection to the United States at the time included the visiting missionaries and occasional Hollywood movies.

Tonga Toutai, Hēhea, Pita, and Tangiteina discussed the move and made a bold decision. They would travel with Vika, the eldest daughter, and leave baby Hēhea who was only a few months old. Tonga Toutai and Hēhea would travel to Salt Lake City for General Conference in a year, and it was agreed they would bring her with them, allowing Pita and Tangiteina to establish themselves in the United States.

Pictures 1950 -1960

The Pāletu'a family. Hēhea, Tangiteina, 'Akesiu, Tonga Toutai. Late 1950's.

The Hihifo District Presidency. From left to right: Fakatou Vaitai, Sovea Kioa, Tonga Toutai and Teiko Fonua.

The Pāletu'a family with Elder Charles Woodworth. Elder Woodworth participated in a boxing match as a missionary to fund a temple trip for the Muti family. He loved the Tongan people. Elder Woodworth would return to Tonga after his first mission with his wife to teach at Liahona High School in 1959-1961 and they would return again to Tonga in 1972-1974 as the Mission President. Tonga Toutai would replace him as Mission President in 1974.

Above: Picture taken in New Zealand with other Tongan families who made the trip in 1958-1959. Below: the children who went on the temple trip with their parents with Elder Woodworth.

Pictures 1950 -1960

Queen Sālote invited Queen Elizabeth to visit Tonga during the latter's coronation and she accepted. She took a tour of the island.

President David O. McKay visited Tonga and prophesied that a Temple would be built in "these islands." A shocking statement considering the remoteness of Tonga from the rest of the world. He is accompanied by a young Elder John Groberg.

Transportation to Tonga was still by boat. Here, President Mckay waving to the crowd that gathered to see him off.

All photos from the Morton Collection.

Liahona College (later High School) was a sign of permanency for the Church in Tonga. The 100 year lease for the property where the school was built was indication to all Tongans that the Church was staying.

The Pāletu'a family lived close to Liahona High School where they could enjoy students, faculty, social events, church meetings and visitors from around the world. Liahona High School also provided tourist experiences in Tonga for people who would visit the islands.

Tangiteina and 'Akesiu at Liahona High School. The school was the center of the community for members of the church where Tonga Toutai and his family would mingle with missionaries, students, and church leaders.

Bottom from left to right: Hēhea, Tangiteina, 'Akesiu and Tonga Toutai. The Pāletu'a family in Liahona. (Kinikini Collection)

Pictures 1950-1960   59

Liahona High School Faculty. December 6, 1956. Front row: Fern Lilywhite, Falupenga Sanft, Metta Header, Lavinia Bird. Middle row: Irene Casper, Lois Humphries, Ermel Morton, Lena Morton, Helen Barrett, Fay Stringham, Zola Jensen. Back row: Viliami Pasi, Filimone Fie'eiki, Reed Garfield, David Stone, Sione Kinikini, Semisi Tonga, Tonga Toutai Pāletu'a, Dale Frost, Semisi Taumoepeau, David Craner, Sione Taufa, Antonio Tui'asoa, Viliami Sovea Kioa. (Morton Collection)

Tonga Toutai's profession as a teacher allowed him to influence young generations of Tongans. (Morton Collection)

Farewells were common in Tonga. Here a group of saints gather to bid farewell. Tonga Toutai can be seen standing next to Ermel Morton and Patrick Dalton on the far left. (Morton Collection)

A boat came once a month with supplies and mail. Here Liahona teachers are in town to pick up mail.

Left to right: Lois Humphries Foutz, Teresa Hadlock, Fern Lillywhite, Zola Jensen. (Morton Collection)

Pictures 1950 -1960   61

The Scouting program in Tonga was boosted by the attendance of a small group of Tongan's to the Scouting Jubilee in Australia. This would be Tonga Toutai's first time traveling outside of the kingdom of Tonga. (Kinikini Collection)

Tonga Toutai (center) learned a lot from his association with teachers and staff at Liahona High School. They were united in the purpose of educating Tongan youth in things both secular and spiritual. (Morton Collection)

Even with the duties of caring for two children, Tonga Toutai and Hēhea stayed involved in their ward and community. Here is Hēhea with young students.

Liahona College (High School) became a center for activities, tourists, dances and church meetings.

The printed program for the dedication of Liahona.

Chapter 5

Missionary Work | 1970 - 1979

But I have prayed for thee, that thy faith fail not: and when thou art converted, strengthen thy brethren.

Luke 22:32

LDS Business College for 'Akesiu

The 1970s brought about much change for the church and Tonga Toutai and Hēhea's family.

Tonga Toutai and Hēhea's commitment to the gospel and building the church in the Kingdom in Tonga were traits they sought to instill in their children. In 1970 'Akesiu traveled with Tonga Toutai to Salt Lake City, Utah. He registered 'Akesiu to attend LDS Business College. The desire was for 'Akesiu to receive an education and perhaps return to the islands to serve the people.

The Need for More Stakes in Tonga

Within three years of the first stake in Tonga being organized, the increase in church membership and leadership experience reached a point where an additional stake was needed. There was a need for more than just one stake. There was a need for three more. By the end of the summer in 1971, there would be four operating stakes of Zion in Tonga.

On July 20, 1971, Elder Howard W. Hunter, accompanied by Brother John H. Groberg, arrived in Tonga to create the new stakes and to reorganize the first stake. Tongan church leaders met that afternoon to discuss boundaries and to make recommendations concerning the

Tonga Toutai and his counselors of the Nuku'alofa (Hihifo) West Stake. (Kinikini Collection)

new Stake Presidents and Patriarchs. Stake Conference was held later that same evening, and Tonga Toutai Pāletu'a was called to be the new stake president. He would be the first Tongan called to this position.

After the completion of the organization, the following was written in the church record:

> This is the result of many years of struggle and persistence by hundreds of faithful saints and missionaries. This has been a great and glorious day in the history of Tonga ("Tonga" 3:2:7).

"Unusual" Leadership

Tonga Toutai was in charge of the Nuku'alofa West Stake. Implementing what he had learned from previous associations with church leaders, his leadership skills, and his dependence on the Lord for guidance, he was able to bless the lives of people in his stake. There was an energy in the work they were doing, and all wanted to be involved. Tonga Toutai reports that he increased his prayers and fasting in order to know what he needed to do. He wanted to be guided by inspiration to help the work move forward.

The Nuku'alofa West Stake was running so well Tonga Toutai received a letter from Salt Lake City from the prophet at the time, Harold B. Lee, noting the faithfulness of the members of the stake on

THE CHURCH OF JESUS CHRIST OF LATTER-DAY SAINTS
47 EAST SOUTH TEMPLE STREET
SALT LAKE CITY, UTAH 84111

HAROLD B. LEE, PRESIDENT

October 8, 1973

HAROLD B. LEE

President Tonga Toutai
Box 102
Nuku'alofa, Tonga

Dear President Toutai:

How pleased we are with the wonderful contribution being made by the Nuku'alofa West Stake toward the building of God's kingdom here upon the earth.

Word comes to us of the outstanding attendance of representatives from your stake at the regional meetings held in August.

We are advised that your stake had perfect attendance of the Primary, Relief Society and Priesthood representatives.

We are aware, Brother Toutai, that such enthusiasm and dedication requires unusual leadership. We extend our sincere commendation to you, your counselors and all who assist.

May our Heavenly Father bless you, with your family, in your teaching at Liahona High School, and in your faithful and effective service to the Church.

Sincerely,

Harold B. Lee

Letter from President Harold B. Lee mentioning his "unusual leadership" skills.

completing their assignments. The prophet used the term, "unusual leadership" to describe what was happening, but Tonga Toutai recorded he was focused on what the Lord wanted him to do to "bless the people." Part of his success as a leader was an intense focus on the scriptures. He desired for the Tongans to realize their true identity as part of the House of Israel and that by obeying God's commandments, Tongans would receive great blessings from the Lord.

While there are no absolute term limits to serving as a stake president, Tonga Toutai would receive a new calling less than three years into this current position. It was a calling that would be a surprise to Tongans and require some "unusual leadership" skills but would ultimately help spread the gospel further among the Tongan people.

Respect for the servants of the Lord

During this time, the kingdom of Tonga received many visitors from Church Headquarters. In addition to his calling as a Stake President, Tonga Toutai was also working at Liahona High School. He was part of the faculty and was also working as the chairman for the committee screening students for entrance to the Church College of Hawaii.

In 1972, Neal A. Maxwell, Commissioner of Education and Elder Delbert L. Stapley, member of the Quorum of the Twelve Apostles, arrived to evaluate the work at Liahona High School. A special devotional was held in the Liahona High School gym. Pakineti Ngatuvai shares the following experience about this event:

> In 1972 there was a devotional at the gym at Liahona. Neal A. Maxwell was there. Elder Stapley was there as well. The students sat facing the stage, and the visiting authorities were on the stage facing the students. In the back of the auditorium, there was a banner that read, "Welcome Elder Neal A. Maxwell, Commissioner of Education for the World" and (below it in smaller print) Elder Stapley. Many observed the banner. After the meeting, Tonga Toutai Pāletu'a was the only one to point out a problem. That the emphasis was welcoming the commissioner and of lesser importance, an Apostle of the Lord.
>
> He told us how embarrassed and sad he was while sitting in the front looking at the banner. He was disappointed that they did not recognize the importance of having an apostle of the Lord among them. He *tafulu'i*

(reprimanded) them for this oversight. It is a memory I have of him and the love and respect he had for the servants of the Lord ("Manatumelie").

Following the Tongan custom of *faka'apa'apa* (respect) for visitors, especially of those of high rank, this was an appropriate rebuke. Tonga Toutai taught them the importance of honoring those called by God in everything.

This example illustrates Tonga Toutai's attention to detail. He observed everything. He evaluated every aspect and made it a priority to be sure things were done correctly. This attention to detail would be helpful four years later when he would be asked to serve as Chairman of the 1976 Area Conference in Tonga. The conference would welcome the prophet and a large group of visiting authorities to Tonga.

'Akesiu's Marriage

In 1973, while 'Akesiu was studying at LDS Business college, she met a Tongan named Tēvita Mapa Vainuku, Jr. They fell in love and were married in the Salt Lake Temple. They remained in the United States and started their family.

Separated and Connected

Tonga Toutai and Hēhea's family were separated by a vast ocean, country, language, and culture, but they retained strong relationships through weekly letters and visits to Utah. Tangiteina and 'Akesiu were both married and living in Salt Lake City. They were both having children and beginning their families. Tonga Toutai and Hēhea were back in Tonga with a very young, Hēhea *si'i* (junior), whom they were raising. Tonga Toutai and Hēhea remained in constant contact with their children through visits to the United States twice a year and weekly letters. Tonga Toutai and Hēhea visited Salt Lake City twice every year for General Conferences held in April and October. During their visits, they would stay with Tangiteina and 'Akesiu, visit with a growing number of grandchildren and help out where they could. In between their visits to Utah, they wrote letters to their daughters every week.

The correspondence from Tonga Toutai and Hēhea to their daughters demonstrated the love and affection a father has for his children. He was concerned for their well-being in the United States.

Tonga Toutai and Hēhea had every opportunity to move to the United States, but they chose to stay in Tonga. Tonga Toutai's patriarchal blessing, given by Eldred Smith in the late 1960s, stated specifically that he was born "away from the stakes of Zion for a wise purpose." In fulfillment of this purpose, they remained in Tonga. This would mean separation from his daughters and grandchildren, but both he and Hēhea knew the Lord would preserve their family if they were obedient.

The Tonga Nuku'alofa Mission

Tonga Toutai's time serving as a stake president would not last long. After only three years, he was called as the new mission president over the Nuku'alofa Tonga Mission.

> The call to be mission president came by telephone from President Spencer W. Kimball on May 5, 1974. The tender sweetness and tone of his voice will stay with me for as long as I live (Shumway 213).

Official mission reports contained the following comment on May 7, 1974:

General Conference allowed the Pāletu'a's an opportunity to meet see their daughters and their families and to associate with people from around the world. Here they are outside of the Tabernacle on Temple Square in-between sessions of General Conference. (Kinikini collection)

President John H. Groberg returned to Tonga with word that President Tonga Toutai Pāletu'a has been called to be the president of the Tonga Mission. This change is to take place immediately, and President Charles J. Woodworth is released.

The time has arrived when the Tongan people are prepared to move ahead and carry the full program of the church. The Lord has revealed to his living prophet that now truly is the time for leaders of Isreal in Tonga to complete the work of gathering Isreal and building the Kingdom of God in this choice land ("Tonga" 3:2:115)

This was the first time a native Tongan would hold this calling.

A few weeks later, on May 21, Elder Thomas S. Monson arrived in Tonga, and along with President Groberg, they set Tonga Toutai apart as the new Mission President over the Nuku'alofa Mission. Hēhea was also set apart by Elder Monson to preside over the mission Primary, Relief Society, Young Women, and the Mutual Improvement Association (MIA). Also called to the mission presidency were William Harris and Herman Wolfgramm.

> My call to be the first native Tongan mission president in Tonga was a shock to some people, but many forces, opportunities, and leaders had prepared me over the years for such a call. I had been a branch president, a district president, a patriarch, and a stake president. Beyond that, I had really never been separated from active missionary teaching since I joined the church. From 1962 to 1968, I had preached regularly for the church on the radio (Shumway 213).

It was a time of celebration. All the missionaries from Vava'u and Ha'apai Districts were brought to Tongatapu to meet Elder Monson and to be interviewed by President Groberg and President Pāletu'a.

The following day, May 22, Elder Monson, President Groberg, and President Pāletu'a met with his Majesty King Taufa'ahau Tupou IV, for about forty-five minutes. Tonga Toutai was officially introduced as the new mission president. President Groberg bore his testimony to the king, who was touched and promised full cooperation with the church and their needs. Tonga Toutai states the following about the experience:

> After the conference in which I was sustained, I accom-

panied Elder Thomas S. Monson and John H. Groberg, then regional representative of the Quorum of the Twelve, to the palace where I was introduced to the king as the first Tongan mission president for the church. I sensed His Majesty's pleasure in the progress among his people that a Tongan should be called to such a position (Shumway 213).

Tonga Toutai immediately focused on the work to be done, and it started with a fast. On May 24, all the missionaries, along with some stake leaders, held a special fast. The purpose of the fast was to receive the Lord's guidance and direction to share the gospel to the Tongan people who had not accepted it.

At the close of the fast, several hundred priesthood leaders met and knelt in prayer. Priesthood leaders of Vava'u and Ha'apai districts also met at the same hour. President Groberg acted as voice in calling upon the Lord to help all the leaders and members in Tonga fully support their newly called leaders and put forth the effort necessary to see that the gospel is taken to every home in Tonga.

> At the appointed time, the priesthood leaders on Tongatapu met in Havelu to break our fast. After a hymn, Elder John Groberg led us in prayer. The Spirit descended mightily on that assembly as Elder Groberg struggled through his tears to call upon the Lord. He could barely utter the words of his prayer. No one could resist the overpowering presence, which bound us together that day. I was as a "prophet in his own country," but I could sense now they all accepted and sustained me as the mission president (213).
>
> There was a burning spirit present, and all left with firm resolves to spread the gospel and build the cause of Zion in Tonga.

Many elements that had been established by former missionary efforts made it possible for the work to grow quickly. With Liahona High School's success, a decision was made to build a new school in Vava'u. On January 4, 1975, Tonga Toutai flew to Vava'u to dedicate the ground for a new school. The new school's name would be Sainehā.

Tonga Toutai's leadership style was firm, and yet he could draw on the characteristics of all the leaders he was able to observe and work with throughout his life. He adjusted to the needs of the individual depending on what would bless their lives and increase results. For example, on February 28, 1975, the following was recorded:

Tonga Toutai held a meeting at 2:00 pm at the mission home to check up on the goals that were set. The president really laid it on the line to them because no one accomplished his goal. All the Zone leaders came out with a new desire ("Tonga" 3:2:123).

Every Detail is Important

As with every call Tonga Toutai received, Hēhea was right there with him, helping to shoulder responsibilities. They were of one mind and one spirit. The work involved both of them, and they worked side by side in every opportunity that came their way.

One example of Hēhea's influence occurred involving the appearance of missionaries. As messengers of the Lord, great attention to how they lived and presented themselves was important. Hēhea worked with other church leaders to implement a new official standard of dress for missionaries in Tonga.

For the Elders, neckties would be of one color as would their *tupenu* (cloth wrap around the waist). They would only wear short sleeve white shirts.

The sisters would all braid their hair in two, one braid on each side of their head, and tied it with a black *loufau* (ribbon) in the back: no bangs or extreme hairstyles. Dresses would be of a single color: no extreme prints - No make-up or lipstick.

Both would wear a black *ta'ovala* (a piece of matting worn around the waist over one's *tupenu*).

> Hēhea worked with the leaders to make these changes…I asked the people I knew in America to send me white shirts, and I would distribute them to the missionaries. If the shirts were long sleeve, we would cut the sleeves so they would be short (Pāletu'a, diary).

Tonga Toutai described the purpose of this change in the following way in his diary, "The change in clothing was for the missionaries to exemplify goodness and encourage behavior equal to their calling."

The changes in missionary wardrobe were more than cosmetic; they were cultural shifts. The new missionary clothing was very Tongan. It conveyed respect to Tonga's cultural heritage and distinctly made missionaries appear less Western. For people who were not members of the church, it was respectful attire. Appropriate for special witnesses

The clothing for missionaries in Tonga remains the same as it was established during President Pāletu'a's time as mission president. Pictured here is Sister Tangiteina Kinikini and Sister Vuki with missionaries from 2007 in Tonga. (Kinikini collection)

anointed to share God's message. The clothing helped missionaries share the gospel to those who viewed Mormonism as an American institution.

While the dress standard was strict, it did not apply to everyone. Foreign missionaries were allowed to choose to wear the Tongan attire or not.

The dress standard for Tongan missionaries continued to be implemented long after their service. While some attempts have been made since that time to change the clothing standard, those attempts have been mostly unsuccessful. The dress standard continues to be used by Tongan missionaries today. It has become synonymous with missionaries from the Church of Jesus Christ to Tongans (Pāletu'a, diary).

The Importance of the Book of Mormon

Tonga Toutai and Hēhea believed the Book of Mormon also contained the ancient history of the Tongan people. They felt their mission was to wake Tongans to the truth of who they were and to the promises God had made to them in the scriptures. They believed that it was only through the Book of Mormon that Tongans could be awakened to their true identity.

There was a mandatory expectation for missionaries to read and teach from the Book of Mormon.

> I organized and encouraged our missionaries to read the Book of Mormon with member families as well as nonmember families. The standing rule for every missionary was to be teaching every night in some home, if not with a nonmember family, then with members, in a family home evening setting. But they must read the Book of Mormon with the family and teach from the Book of Mormon (Shumway 214).

Tonga Toutai stated that up until that time, missionaries taught mostly from the Bible.

> Most Tongan members over the years have been uncomfortable teaching from a book not commonly accepted by other Christians. In fact, they have been afraid to use it or to even mention it in the presence of nonmembers (214).

Change is not easy for everyone. The focus for missionaries to read and teach from the Book of Mormon was still challenging for some missionaries. One particular missionary did not follow through with reading the Book of Mormon. However, from this disobedience came a humorous event that produced more obedience from other missionaries.

> I remember in one meeting with the missionary leaders, I instructed them to read the Book of Mormon again. I had done it in four nights of intense reading. They were to read it again and to make sure when they ever spoke in church, to preach from the Book of Mormon. Well, one of my zone leaders did not take my instructions seriously since his time as a missionary was concluded. When I released him at the scheduled time, somehow, word mistakenly got out to the missionaries that his release was a disciplinary action for not reading and teaching from the Book of Mormon. From then on, there wasn't one missionary who failed to study the Book of Mormon faithfully (Shumway 214).

A Focus on Gathering Israel

The fervor of missionary work was deeply rooted in Tonga Toutai's belief in gathering lost Israel. His ideas about Tongan's being a part of lost Israel can be found in an article he wrote for the December 1975 edition of the Ensign magazine titled, "I Could Not Hold Back the Tears." In the article, he states:

> I know without a doubt, the Book of Mormon is a second witness of the Savior, the Son of God, Jesus Christ, the head of this church. The Book of Mormon contains the fullness of the gospel and the true history of my ancestors. This people have been named Tongans by men, but I am proud when I use the name given us by the Lord - Lamanites. My skin may be brown and dark in color, but I know assuredly that my blood is pure and perfect, for it is the blood of Nephi, Lehi, Manasseh, Joseph, Jacob, Isaac, and Abraham.
>
> It is my goal to have my brothers eat of the Tree of Life, like my ancestor Lehi desired for his sons. I desire my people to eat of this tree; to take a Book of Mormon to every home in this land and to all the children of Lehi, the nobles and the commoners, the house of Israel, the beloved children of our Heavenly Father, to gather them all to Zion for Tonga are all Stakes of Zion.

His conviction in sharing the gospel to his fellow countrymen inspired his missionaries to do the same. He also promised his missionaries that if they were obedient and faithful, they would be blessed and witness miracles during their missions.

Invitations to preach in other churches

The excitement and dedication of the missionaries opened doors. Soon the Lord provided opportunities for the missionaries to share the gospel in places they were usually not welcome; at the pulpit of other churches.

The following is taken from Tonga Toutai's recorded history:

> I was surprised to receive a written invitation from the president of the Wesleyan church for me to come and speak with my missionaries in *Saione* (Zion) about the

Book of Mormon... I gathered all the missionaries, and we traveled to *Saione*. The church was full of people. Our missionaries sang the "Year of the Lamanite" song. We also brought along 150 Books of Mormon. We distributed all the books to the people, and I bore my testimony.

The next day after that meeting, I received another invitation from a man named Semisi Koloto, a preacher in Longolongo. I went there with the missionaries and taught there as well. I taught from the Bible and from the Book of Mormon and told them they were the descendants of Laman and Nephi. The missionaries sang, and we distributed more copies of the Book of Mormon to the people. This was historic (Pāletu'a, diary).

The culmination of decades worth of missionary work transitioned perceptions of the church from distrust to friendship. A new era for missionary work was dawning. During Tonga Toutai's lifetime, he witnessed dramatic changes in the way the gospel was being received and embraced in the kingdom of Tonga.

Open House in Sopu

The mission effort was not only restricted to visiting people in their homes, villages, and churches. They also invited investigators to come to the mission home in Sopu. Tonga Toutai shared the following in Tongan Saints: Legacy of Faith:

One of the greatest moments in our missionary service occurred at a special open house in the mission home on April 27, 1975. By design, the missionaries brought all of their golden contacts with the understanding there would be a baptism at the conclusion of the program. The place was teeming with people, and we had to use every room. The open house extended almost until midnight, but the end result was forty-four baptisms in one night (Shumway 214).

Stake in Vava'u

In less than ten years since the first stake was organized in the kingdom of Tonga, another stake was being created, this time in Vava'u.

President Pāletu'a with missionaries during a zone conference.

In 1975 Elder Gordon B. Hinckley and Elder John H. Groberg arrived to establish a stake in Vava'u. It was a joyous occasion for all.

> The Lord has blessed the people in all the areas of Tonga, from the big islands to the small. The gospel is moving forward in Tonga (Paletu'a, diary).

The Temple is our Goal

The growth of missionary work and the establishment of stakes excited the Tongan saints to work toward receiving their temple ordinances. Faithful members worked hard, saved money, and sacrificed much to plan family trips to the Temple in New Zealand. They traveled in groups, much like Tonga Toutai had done with his family in 1949. These small groups would travel together and care for each other much like the pioneers from the United States while crossing the plains. They were united in purpose and shared all they could to help each other reach the temple. By the end of 1975, five groups of Tongan saints would make the trip to the New Zealand Temple to receive their ordinances and perform them for their ancestors. The temple was always the goal.

Ta'u oe Kau Leimana

The Tonga Nuku'alofa Mission had gone through many changes in just a few years; a change in missionary attire, focus on the Book of Mormon, speaking in different churches, open houses in the mission home. These efforts created excitement among the missionaries and members. In 1976, the mission instituted a theme for all the missionaries. It was called *Ta'u oe kau Leimana* or "Year of the Lamanite."

The missionary work during this period in Tonga was astounding. Missionaries were asked to vigorously study the Book of Mormon every day, pray often for guidance, fast frequently, and share the gospel with everyone. They were asked to memorize passages of scriptures so they could easily teach with the Spirit. Tonga Toutai focused on the Book of Mormon as an authentic ancient history of the Tongan people. He championed the doctrine taught in the Book of Mormon and preached from it often.

The missionaries were encouraged to reach out in various ways, including performing dramas from themes of the Book of Mormon and performing musical numbers. Songs were composed.

The missionaries who served during this time share a unique bond. The missionaries from this era continue to keep in touch. They have a Facebook social media group where they share stories and memories. They also hold reunions every year and gather to share remembrances of their missionary work. The reunions are elaborate three-day events with feasts, speeches, traditional performances, and a fireside. The memories they share coincide with how much their missionary experience has influenced the trajectory of their lives. The memories and experiences of the missionaries who served during this time could fill another book. It would be impossible to include it here.

1976 Area Conference

The purpose of an Area Conference was to bring General Conference to the members of the church who lived far away from Utah. The president of the church and other general authorities traveled to the people to provide a conference experience. While radio technology existed to share General Conference, it remained limited to the areas of the world that had an infrastructure that could support it. In places as remote as Tonga, General Conference would often take months to reach the saints. The blessing of having the prophet and other church

The Area Conference visitors arriving in Tonga. Tonga Toutai is in front walking with President Spencer W. Kimball and his wife, Camilla. (Kinikini collection)

leaders visit such remote places was a show of love for saints throughout the world.

The first Tongan area conference of the Church of Jesus Christ of Latter-day Saints was held on Tuesday and Wednesday, February 24-25, 1976. Six sessions were scheduled during the two-day conference. All the sessions were held at Liahona High School.

Tonga Toutai was in charge of the planning committee for the conference in addition to his responsibilities as Mission President. He, along with committee members, planned everything carefully. The traveling group of Church leaders coming for the Area Conference was large, and their care and well-being while in Tonga was essential because they would continue to travel to various Area Conferences around the world. Their visit to Tonga was brief, and careful attention to time was going to be of paramount importance. Tonga Toutai's focus was to ensure everything was in order so the Tongan people could experience General Conference the way he and Hēhea had experienced it in Salt Lake City. The committee and their spouses fasted and prayed for guidance.

The Tongan members of the church were excited to receive the prophet and other general authorities. Attending the conference were: President Spencer W. Kimball, President N. Eldon Tanner, of the First Presidency; Elder Bruce R. McConkie and Elder David B. Haight of the Council of the Twelve Apostles; Elder Marion Duff Hanks, Elder William H. Bennett, Elder Robert L. Simpson, Elder Robert D. Hales of the Assistants to the Twelve; Elder Loren C. Dunn of the First Council of the Seventy, Presiding Bishop Victor L. Brown; President Russell M. Nelson, general president of the Sunday School; Sister Sara Tanner, wife of President N. Eldon Tanner; and Brother D'Monte W. Coombs, area conference coordinator, as well as local mission, stake, ward and branch leaders.

All preparations for the conference were made by a local planning committee under the direction of Tonga Toutai, President of the Tonga Nuku'alofa mission. Members of this planning committee were: Tēvita Ka'ili, Sione T. Lātū, Vaikalafi Lutui, Pita Hopoate, Vili Pele Folau, Viliami Harris, Tēvita Folau Mahu'inga, and Viliami Sika.

Amid the celebrations, the Tongan saints were eager to hear the words of the prophet. The topic of missionary work was also discussed. President Kimball emphasized the need for church members to spread the gospel and build the kingdom in their own land. The Tongan saints were to build Zion in Tonga.

Tongan Missionaries to other Lands

As church membership grew, more and more Tongans wanted to serve missions. In 1977 and 1978, more applicants desired to serve a mission than there were positions in Tonga to fill. The only option was to begin sending Tongan missionaries outside of Tonga. In 1978, six Tongans were sent to Bolivia; twelve to the Philippines; four were called to Fiji, and a few more were sent to Hawaii (Britsch 487).

Regional Representative for the Twelve Apostles

1977 brought new responsibilities. While presiding over the Tonga Nuku'alofa Mission, Tonga Toutai was called to serve as the Regional Representative of the Twelve Apostles for the Kingdom Island of Tonga. Tahiti would later be added to this assignment.

Beginning on May 5, 1977, until 1980, Tonga Toutai would travel throughout the Pacific, fulfilling responsibilities and following up on assignments in those areas. During this assignment, Tonga Toutai learned how to communicate in basic French. He was familiar with the Lord's work in Tonga, and he also became familiar with the Lord's work in Samoa and Tahiti.

At the end of his work as a Regional Representative for the Twelve, he received a letter of appreciation on November 9, 1981. In part, it reads:

We are grateful, Brother Pāletu'a, for the outstanding service you have rendered as a Regional Representative these past few years. You have influenced many lives and have fully demonstrated your devotion and loyalty to the church, to your fellowmen, and to the Lord. The insight you have gained in this position will enable you to render even more effective service to the master. With your knowledge and background, you should be a strong force in urging the priesthood to magnify their callings.

Through your long experience in Church service, you have learned of the great blessings of having devoted and reliable coworkers to share the burdens and responsibilities entrusted to your care. With this insight, you can better appreciate the good feelings which the First Presidency and the Quorum of the Twelve have toward you for the selfless way in which you have served, thereby easing their load and helping to advance the Lord's work (Pāletu'a, diary).

Tonga Toutai traveled to Salt Lake City to attend every general conference and report on the work in the Pacific. It was during his visit in 1980 that Tonga Toutai learned the Lord had more substantial plans for the saints in Tonga and that church president David O. McKay's words from 1955 would be fulfilled.

Chapter 6

The Temple | 1980 - 1989

*For behold, I have accepted this house, and my name shall be here;
and I will manifest myself to my people in mercy in this house.*
Doctrine and Covenants 110:7

A New Temple in Tonga

Tonga Toutai was serving as a Regional Representative to the Twelve Apostles serving the areas of Tonga and Tahiti during the beginning of the 1980s.

Tonga Toutai was informed about the Temple in Tonga before it was officially announced to the church during the April General Conference. He wrote the following regarding this experience in his diary:

> Wednesday, April 2, 1980 - There was a meeting in the First Presidency's office, and President Tanner conducted... also in attendance was President Romney, The Temple Committee and... Elder Packer. The Prophet, Spencer W. Kimball, announced that there would be a temple in Nuku'alofa, Tahiti, Samoa, and Australia. I was overjoyed that I was able to hear this news. There has been much prayer and fasting among the Tongan people for this very thing. I was given time to represent the six Stake Presidents of Tonga and the people and Stake President of Tahiti. I thanked the Prophet and his counselors, as well as the Twelve Apostles and all the leaders of the church in the world. This was the most important blessing given to Tonga, such a small island in the sea (Pāletu'a, journal).

The Nuku'alofa Tonga Temple would be the 23rd functioning Temple in the latter-day dispensation. It would also fulfill the prophecy given by President David O. McKay during his visit to Tonga in 1955 where he said he saw a temple "in these islands."

Tonga Toutai was given new responsibilities in addition to his current callings. He was called to be the Committee Chairman of the Temple Dedication and Celebration ceremonies. This included everything related to the groundbreaking ceremonies.

It would take several years before the construction of the temple would be completed, but Tonga Toutai's enthusiasm never waned. He lived across the street from the Temple site. He was able to observe the building of the Temple daily and felt blessed to be living within its shadow.

Clearing the Land

There was excitement among the members of the church in Tonga regarding the new temple. Preparing the land for the building of the temple was a joint effort. Initially, a smaller group worked in clearing the land, and then the second wave of members volunteered to do the rest of the work.

Tonga Toutai recorded the following in his journal about clearing the land.

> January 28, 1981 - We began clearing the land of Tēvita Folau Mahu'inga, which was set apart for the building of the Holy House of the Lord, the temple. We used Tu'imana Mateaki's plow and the weed cutter from Makeke. The following people worked on clearing the land that day. Tonga Toutai Pāletu'a, Sione Tu'alau Latu, Sosiua Teiko Fonua, Vaikalafi Lutui and his family, Sione Leisi and his family, Tēvita Lutui and his family. There were twenty-seven of us.

On January 31, 1981, he recorded the following:

> Members from the five stakes in Tonga converged to continue clearing the land. We began with a song and a prayer. I presided over the meeting. Vaikalafi Lutui conducted. We began work at 7:00 am, and we ended at noon. There were approximately 2,000 workers. The Liahona Stake divided work among the different wards.

The number of members that showed up to help clear the land for the temple from the different stakes in Tonga made the task easy and quick. The work had only taken a few hours to complete. Tonga Toutai recorded in his journal that the mood of the people that day was happiness and joy.

Groundbreaking

Tonga Toutai writes the following about the groundbreaking ceremonies in his diary:

> February 18, 1981 - The Prophet Spencer W. Kimball arrived with others to dedicate the ground where the Holy Temple will be built. The arrival of President Kimball is a momentous occasion for the Tongan people. President Kimball blessed the site. The King of Tonga, Tupou V. Queen Halaevalu Mata'aho, nobles from different islands, ministers, and officials from the government attended. There were also many people who attended the dedication (ceremonies). Approximately 7,000 people attended. The groundbreaking and site dedication

President Kimball and other officials at the ground breaking ceremony. (Burgoyne Collection) Feb 22, 1981

began at 2:00 in the afternoon. Elder Komatsu conducted the ceremony...A welcome was prepared at Liahona High School. Celebrations were held at the neighboring Liahona High School with traditional dances, singing, and oratorical presentations... The temple will soon bless us in the far islands of the sea.

Tonga Toutai felt a special bond between President Kimball during this visit. President Kimball seemed to emanate love in the way he interacted with the people and in his behavior. The people of Tonga felt it, and so did Tonga Toutai. He records the following in his diary:

> At all times the prophet would see me he would ask me to come to him and to sit with him. He spoke to me and said, "I love you very much." He would then hold my hand, and he would repeat what he said. I told him that I loved him too. He asked me if I was born in Tonga, and I said, "Yes."

In the same diary entry, Tonga Toutai also recorded an interesting observation about the King of Tonga, Tupou IV, and the prophet.

> After all the ceremonies were done, the King returned

to the Palace, but before he left, he told me that he felt a strong feeling of love for the prophet of the Lord. I told him President Kimball is a prophet, a man of God with the gift of prophecy.

Calling as the Temple President

The following from Lanier Britsch's book, *Unto the Islands of the Sea: A History of the Latter-day Saints in the Pacific*, is of particular interest about the groundbreaking ceremonies.

> Generally, the Brethren have called an experienced member from the United States as the first president of a foreign temple. But while President Kimball was in Tonga for the groundbreaking, he felt inspired to call Brother Pāletu'a to that position. President Kimball asked Pāletu'a to see him when he came to General Conference in April 1981. The call was extended at that time (494).

Tonga Toutai recalled the following about receiving the call as Temple President:

> On February 21, (1981), after the visitors from Salt Lake City returned, the prophet called me and said, "Hello, Elder Pāletu'a. How are you?" I responded, "I am fine, thank you, President." Then he said to me, "You remember the Temple in Tonga? I call you to be the president of the Tonga Temple. Do you accept the call?" I responded, "Yes, President Kimball, very fine." Then he said, "You choose your first and second counselors and bring them to my office on a note." I said, "Yes, I will come next week, on the 25th, Wednesday." Then he said, "Yes, remember to drop in my office." We said good-bye, and then I spoke with his secretary, Brother Haycock, "*Malo-e-lelei*. Are you coming for the conference?" "Yes." "Ok. Good luck. I will see you then (Pāletu'a, diary)."

The profoundness of this moment was overwhelming. Tonga Toutai had received the calling as the new Temple President over the telephone in a short, matter-of-fact conversation with the prophet. He shared the following after the phone call:

> I was overwhelmed and felt of my own personal weak-

nesses, but I also felt deep joy. I could not speak as I recalled hearing the humble prophet's voice touch me to my soul. I stood up and went to Hēhea and Patiola. I told them I had just been called as the first president of the Tonga Temple. We did not speak. We returned home without saying a word. We knelt down and gave our deepest thanks and gratitude to the Lord (Pāletu'a, diary).

Tonga Toutai and Hēhea prepared for the trip to Salt Lake City for the April General Conference. He had prayed for guidance to know who the Lord wanted as counselors. He had the names ready and on a piece of paper when they arrived in Utah. He continues:

On March 30, I went with Pita, my son-in-law, to the office of the prophet... we spent an hour and a half there. The prophet called in his counselors, and they come to his office, and we met with them, even President Romney. We also learned while we were there that President Reagan was shot, he is the president of the United States. It was an important day for me and Pita, my son. We visited the prophet for a long time. He counseled Pita, and I also met with him alone. He is the chosen of God. We received a witness that he is the true prophet of God (Pāletu'a, diary).

Actual Construction on the Temple

It would take seven and a half months before construction on the temple would begin. Tonga Toutai wrote the following in his journal:

October 1, 1981 - The Temple construction contractor arrived in Tonga. His name is Aaron Wilfred Hansen. He arrived with his wife. Also arriving was Richard Nelson Westover, the representative from the church in charge of Temples and Special Projects. He arrived with his wife to oversee the construction. The official construction began on October 2, 1981. They first worked on removing the remaining coconut trees and leveling the land. Work continued to be done in extracting the root of coconut trees and clearing the land.

It was during this time that Tonga Mohenoa Folau and Sione Mateaki were hired, and they began working on building a place for the building equipment and a place for the labor missionaries to live.

> November 2, 1981 - Eighteen missionaries were called to begin working on construction in addition to the fifteen additional paid workers. The work was divided, and the missionaries were placed in different groups to work. Work was slow and tedious (Pāletu'a, diary).

Vainuku Family Returns to Tongatapu

In 1981 Tangiteina and 'Akesiu received word that Hēhea Sr. was ill. 'Akesiu and her husband returned to Tonga with all of their children. During their visit, 'Akesiu had a dream that prompted her to return to the islands. They returned to the United States, where they had another child and then decided as a family to move back to Tonga. They packed up their things and moved.

They were able to ease into life in Tonga and with Tonga Toutai and Hēhea quickly. Tēvita Mapa found work as a teacher at Liahona High School. The Vainuku family would remain in Tonga for many years as

Tēvita Mapa, 'Akesiu and Vaikalafi Lutui. (Kinikini Collection)

their family grew. They would have six more children in Tonga. They also lived a few houses away from Tonga Toutai and Hēhea (Vaisa "'Akesiu Interview").

Hurricane Isaac

The building of the temple did not go without some obstacles. Tonga Toutai writes the following in his journal:

> March 3, 1982 - A violent hurricane hit the island. 'They've named it Hurricane Isaac. There was not one thing that was damaged on the Temple property. All the work that had been completed thus far was not harmed. The Lord protected the temple just as President Kimball had asked during the dedication when he asked the Lord to protect the temple from natural disasters. The roof from the labor missionary home and the roof from the equipment shed were blown off. After the hurricane, they were rebuilt.
>
> The hurricane is difficult for the island. Many people are destitute and struggling. Despite the difficulty, the work continues on the temple. Bricks are being laid; the foundation is being wired for electricity and plumbing. The work continues forward.

Hurricane Isaac also had unintended consequences in that it increased visibility for the church. Disasters brought about opportunities for service. The members of the church, perhaps excited by the new temple, eagerly found ways to serve people. The Church in Salt Lake allocated a million dollars of relief funds plus shipments of material goods to help the Tongans. Members worked to obtain church assistance, which helped to reconstruct homes. It was reported that "the whole population (of Tonga) was so impressed by the Church members and the welfare program that missionary work surged forth opening doors for missionary work (Britsch 490).

Building a Temple in Tonga is Hard Work

As construction moved forward, the labor missionaries worked tirelessly to complete the temple despite the difficulties. Tonga Toutai writes the following about the labor missionaries in his diary:

Concrete blocks were pushed up this ramp in wheelbarrels to build the temple. (Tuione Collection)

During May (1982), the labor missionaries were working very diligently. They were asked to deliver concrete blocks up to the tower by pushing them up a ramp in wheel barrels. It was very difficult work.

The rafters and roof of the temple were constructed off-site first. They were added to the building after the walls were completed. During this time, landscaping was added to the Temple site. The work is beautiful to behold.

Welcome, Brother

Amid the building of the temple, another miracle was happening. The decades of spiritual separation between Tonga Toutai and his family was sweetened by a surprise visit from one of his older brothers.

As Viliami Pāletu'a had done, his son, 'Ulamoleka, chose to dedicate his life as a *faifekau* in Vava'u. After years of preaching and Bible study, he woke up one day and knew the Church of Jesus Christ of Latter-day Saints was true. He left his ministry immediately, without communicating with anyone, and traveled to Tongatapu to see his brother.

When he arrived, he told his brother that he knew the church was true. He asked his younger brother to baptize him. On July 31, 1982,

Tonga Toutai's brother, 'Ulamoleka, is baptized a member of the church on July 31, 1982.

Tonga Toutai's brother, 'Ulamoleka Pāletu'a, became a member of the Church of Jesus Christ of Latter-Day Saints.

Only one other sibling in the Pāletu'a family would join the church, a sister, Malama.

Temple President Training in Salt Lake City

On September 28-30, a training for twenty-seven temple presidents and their wives gathered at the Jordan River Temple in Salt Lake City, Utah.

President Ezra Taft Benson of the Quorum of the Twelve concluded the training sessions by emphasizing the importance of the calling they held. He also counseled "the presidents and their wives to have complete love and unity at all times, nurturing a spirit of peace and love of the Savior in their homes." ("Seminar" 1982)

Placing the Angel Moroni on top of the tonga Temple. (Tuione Collection)

The Angel Moroni

The pinnacle of LDS Temples is the placement of the Angel Moroni statue atop the spire, which is a symbol of the gathering of Israel in the latter-days in preparation for the return of the Savior. The arrival of the Angel Moroni was a joyous occasion for all the saints. Tonga Toutai wrote the following in his journal:

January 1983 - We began finishing work on the tower. On January 8, the Angel Moroni was placed atop the Temple tower. There were many people gathered around for the occasion. We began to sing, "An Angel from on High" and "We Thank Thee O God for a Prophet" as we watched the Angel Moroni being placed on the temple. We all wept.

It was something the Tongan people had never seen. The Angel Moroni was flying just like the everlasting gospel. It was broadcast over the radio throughout Tonga. It is a testimony of the Tongan people that they are a part of 'God's love, which extends from Abraham, Isaac, Jacob, Joseph, Manasseh, and then through Lehi to the Tongan people.

Placing the Angel Moroni on the temple made the temple appear more beautiful and complete.

Elder Groberg taking King George Taufa'ahau IV on a tour of the temple. (Tuione Collection)

Open House

Preparations for the open house and dedication of the temple began after construction on the temple was completed. On June 12-13, 1983, a fast was held throughout Tonga to prepare for the dedication of the temple. Tonga Toutai records in his journal that he ended his fast on this day.

Church membership increased during the construction of the temple. Before the open house, Elder Howard W. Hunter of the Quorum of the Twelve Apostles and Elder John H. Groberg were in Tonga to establish new units in Pangai, 'Ha'apai. Tonga Toutai mentioned in his journal that the increase in membership was attributed mainly to interest in the temple.

After construction was completed, Tonga Toutai received the physical keys to the temple from Brother Mahoney and Brother Westover. He then conducted a tour of the Temple with Elder Hunter, Elder Groberg, all the stake presidents of Tonga and the Temple Committee.

On July 9, 1983, the temple was opened for the King of Tonga, Taufa'ahau Tupou IV, and the queen, Halaevalu Mata'aho. Elder John H. Groberg conducted the tour of the building. Accompanying them in the group were nobles and government leaders. The group stopped in

Elder Groberg, President Pāletu'a, Elders Hinckley, Hunter, Ashton and Perry after the first dedication services outside of the Nuku'alofa, Tonga Temple. (Tuione Collection)

an Endowment room, the baptismal font, and the Celestial Room. Elder Groberg explained to them gospel principles. Tonga Toutai recorded, "The Temple is a house of order, and it is beautiful." Following this tour of the temple, a celebration was held at Liahona High School, where the King of Tonga received a statue as a gift.

The public open house for the temple was held on July 18-30, 1983. Tonga Toutai recorded that the open house was busy and that people traveled long distances to attend. He also recorded that many festivals and celebrations occurred during this time. It was during this time that he received names from Salt Lake City to be performed in the temple after the dedication.

Prisoners Shall Go Free

John H. Groberg shared the following experience during the open house of the temple he experienced with Tonga Toutai Paletu'a, in his book, Anytime, Anywhere. The following is taken directly from his book.

> Jean and I conducted many VIP tours of the temple. The people who went through included the King and Queen, members of the Royal Family, government leaders, and officials from other churches, among others. There were dozens of tours, and an amazing number of Tongans visited the temple. What heartwarming and eternally significant conversations as we had! As with all temple open houses, questions were asked, prayers were answered, hearts were touched, and eternal truths were explained. As a result, seeds of truth were planted, and many long-buried testimonies were reawakened. We collected an abundance of referrals, and many people joined the church largely because of what they experienced at the open house.
>
> Of the many groups, we conducted through the temple open house, one in particular, will forever be etched in my heart. At that time, the nation of Tonga was generally peaceful, with very little violent crime. Occasionally someone got drunk and raised some havoc, but for the most part, society was quite tranquil. There were no prisons as we know them, just designated enclosures with a single strand of barbed wire surrounding them. Many of the inmates were there because they had failed to pay their taxes or committed some other similar violation. Often people were sent to prison to work in

government gardens until their debts were paid. So, in a sense, the inmates were not really "criminals," as we use the term.

Without my knowledge, President Tonga Toutai Paletu'a, who had been called by President Spencer W. Kimball to be the temple's first president, had made arrangements with one of the wardens to bring a group of these so-called "prisoners" to an open house tour. Other than their casual attire and the presence of a couple of unarmed guards with them, they appeared much like the other groups going through the open house.

Toward the end of the day, I was taking a group through when I noticed President Paletu'a and his group. I was a little surprised, but felt no concern, as I had full confidence in him. After I finished with my group, I looked around the temple to see if I could find President Paletu'a and his group. I found them in the baptismal area. The scene that I witnessed was so spiritually penetrating that I could hardly move or even breathe. The display of beauty emanating from this group that it transfixed me right where I stood.

The "prisoners" were standing in the back aisle facing the baptismal font. President Paletu'a was speaking to them. Their eyes were fastened on him. They were listening with complete attention and deep reverence as he read from Doctrine and Covenants 128:22: "Courage, brethren;...Let your hearts rejoice, and be exceedingly glad... for the prisoners shall go free." When he finished reading, he bore testimony, then stood there with great power and majesty. All of the men, including the guards, were in tears there in the Lord's house. As I looked at that group of "prisoners," I could literally feel their belief in the truths that had just been explained. They truly wanted to be free - in more ways than one - and they knew that through the Savior's atonement and resurrection, and by obedience to gospel ordinances and principles, they could be. Their gratitude for the Savior and the path laid out for them, along with their determination to obey Him, was as strong as a pulsating heartbeat and could not be denied.

I probably should have closed the door and stepped out, but I couldn't. I was glued to the spot by the marvelous light of truth and gratitude for the Savior flowing so freely from those in that room. In a way, I sensed that this scene and these feelings were but a prelude of things to come - here and hereafter. It was as though I was in an element beyond this world. It was so beautiful and so satisfying that I wished it would last forever.

I'm not sure when they left the room, for the reverent hush continued as the "prisoners" and their guards filed out to their waiting vans. Each one expressed deep, heartfelt appreciation for all they had seen, heard, and felt. I watched President Paletu'a shaking hands and giving hugs to the departing group. He looked like an angel - confidently standing in humble dignity, dressed in white, smiling, encouraging, uplifting. He knew he had followed the promptings of the Lord's Spirit and done that which the Savior would have done, had He been there. From the look in President Paletu'a's eyes and the glow from his very being, I knew in a way He had been.

Years later, I asked President Paletu'a if he had followed through with the men from the prison. He reported that the few who had been less-active members of the church at the time were now active. The others had been baptized and were likewise active. Truly, the Lord performs wonders in mysterious ways. How grateful I was to have been permitted to stand on the periphery and catch a glimpse of the towering testimony of those faithful descendants of Joseph (Groberg "Anytime, Anywhere" 65-68).

Dedication

The Nuku'alofa Tonga Temple was dedicated on August 9, 1983, by President Gordon B. Hinckley from the First Presidency. President Hinckley was accompanied by Elder Marvin J. Ashton, Elder L. Tom Perry, Elder W. Grant Bangerter, Elder John H. Groberg, and Bishop H. Burke Petersen. Dedication services continued from August 9 to August 11.

During the dedicatory prayer, President Hinckley stated the following:

> We thank Thee for all of thy faithful saints in these beautiful islands and invoke Thy blessings upon them that they may be blessed with love and peace in their homes, that their lands shall be productive, that they shall be prospered in their righteous undertakings, that they shall be protected from the storms of nature and from the conflicts of men if they will walk in obedience to Thy commandments... Now we meet together, Father, on this most glorious occasion in the long history of Thy

work in these beautiful islands, to dedicate unto Thee and unto Thy Son this sacred temple (Pāletu'a, diary).

Temple Work Begins Immediately

Ordinances in the temple began immediately following the dedication ceremonies. Tonga Toutai recorded in his journal that Baptisms for the Dead commenced on August 11. Endowment sessions for the dead began on August 11 as well as the first Temple marriage. Living endowments and family sealings for living persons began on August 12. Sealings for deceased families began on August 15. The temple was active from the beginning. By the end of December of that year, 470 people had received their own endowment in the temple.

The Paletu'a Family Together

Temples are about family, and it seemed fitting that the dedication of the Tonga Temple brought together all of Tonga Toutai and Hēhea's posterity. Pita and Tangiteina carefully planned and saved money to afford a trip back to Tonga with all nine of their children ranging in ages

'Akesiu and Tangiteina with their husbands and some of their children during the Temple dedication. Left to right: Tēvita Mapa, Seini, 'Akesiu, Hēhea, Tonga, Vika, Tangiteina, Mele, Pita. (Kinikini collection)

from fifteen to two years old. 'Akesiu and Tēvita Mapa were already in Tonga with their children. It was the first time the entire family was all together since Tangiteina and Pita had moved to the United States in 1969. It was a joyous occasion for the entire family.

One Year Celebration

Tongans traditionally hold a large celebration for a child after their first year of life. The completion of a child's first year of life is an important marker. Traditional Tongan custom rarely celebrated yearly birthdays, as in Western culture; however, Tongans do throw elaborate celebrations for the first birthday of a child. Especially if the child is the firstborn. (Morton 1996) In keeping with Tongan culture, the first birthday of the temple was a marker, and a celebration was held in front of the temple.

In 1984, Elders L. Tom Perry of the Twelve Apostles and Ron Simpson traveled to Tonga to celebrate the first year of the Temple in Tonga. The event was celebrated with singing, performances, and even a cake. The temple had not only survived during the first year, but it also flourished. The temple had been busy with no signs of slowing down. The Tongan people had finally received their temple.

Tonga Toutai and Hēhea served as Temple President and Matron from 1983 until 1987.

Pictures 1960 - 1980

With a new baby. From left to right: Hēhea, Vika, 'Akesiu, Tangiteina and Pita.

Tonga Toutai kept busy in callings at church and also with responsiblities at school.

The new baby was exciting for the family.

Tonga Toutai would travel to Salt Lake City for General Conferences. The first few times in the latter part of the 1960's, he would meet many church leaders and make new friends. He met David O. McKay, the wife of Joseph Fielding Smith and many others. During the 1968 visit, they invited N. Eldon Tanner to the Mission Jubilee celebration in Tonga. The Jubilee celebration was under the direction of Mission President John H. Groberg. He accepted and joined the saints in Tonga for that occasion.

Tonga Toutai kept a busy schedule and worked hard to serve. His association with other great men shaped his leadership style. He learned compassion, determination, how to follow through, how to speak and behave with royalty from wonderful Tongan and papālangi men who taught him.

Elders Howard W. Hunter and Thomas S. Monson arriving in Tonga to establish a stake. You can see Tonga Toutai and Hēhea following behind them.

Teenagers, Tangiteina and 'Akesiu in their Liahona school uniforms.

President Spencer W. Kimball would visit Tonga multiple times. This is a photo of his visit during the 1976 Area Conference. The Area Conference was an opportunity to bring the General Conference to the people of the world. Today, General Conference is broadcast throughout the world via satellite, television, radio and the internet.

In 1974, Tonga Toutai was called to be the Mission President of the Nuku'alofa, Tonga Mission after only serving as a Stake President for a few years.

Tonga Toutai and Hēhea visited Salt Lake City, Utah at least twice a year for General Conference. They would also travel to Utah for training meetings. While in Salt Lake City, they would visit and stay with their daughter, Tangiteina and 'Akesiu who were both living in Utah with their families.

Increased membership required the building of more chapels. Groundbreaking ceremonies like these happened often. It also included groundbreaking for a new school in Vava'u, which would be called Saineha.

Pictures 1960 - 1980   105

A much older and weaker President Kimball would arrive for the groundbreaking ceremonies for the Nuku'alofa Tonga Temple. Tonga Toutai lead the committee for the groundbreaking ceremonies.

Elder Robert L. Simpson, director of the church's social services visited the islands and became fast friends with Tonga Toutai. They exchanged letters with each other about work in the church and to follow up on how each was doing

Among the General Authorities who visited during the 1976 Area Conference was a young Russell M. Nelson. He was serving as the President of the Sunday School for the church. He would return many more times as an apostle and as a prophet.

Pictures 1960 - 1980 **107**

Tongan church leadership are pictured here with President Kimball and his wife and Elder Adney Komatsu and his wife. Tongan priesthood leaders are also pictured.

President Kimball's arrival for the 1976 Area Conference was a welcome fit for royalty. The rain had fallen heavily for days and the ground was wet but the saints were happy to perform as they had been preparing for week. Later, a letter from N. Eldon Tanner would ask Tonga Toutai to pass on his apologies to the performers who performed despite the rain.

Temple work for Tonga Toutai's parents and family members were performed in the Salt Lake Temple as soon as it was possible to perform them.

Here is Tangiteina and Hēhea near the church office building in Salt Lake City, Utah.

The mission of Tonga requires a lot of traveling between islands. Tonga Toutai and Hēhea sacrificed much to be sure the missionaries and the missionary effort were going well.

Hēhea was a powerful influence in helping the work move forward. Working together with church leaders they instituted a dress code for missionaries. The dress code helped the missionary feel in tune to their work and was also appropriate within the context of Tongan culture.

Attempts have been made to change the dress standard since this time but they have been met with opposition by members, missionaries and Tongans. It remains in place today.

Hēhea with her parents, Tevita Kona'i and Mosiana Ngatū during a celebration. The Kona'ī family were very close.

Missionary work during Tonga Toutai and Hēhea's time saw miracles. They were invited to preach in other churches and during one Christmas, 44 souls entered the waters of baptism on the same night.

Tongan life requires a lot of demands on time. The Lord blessed Tonga and Hēhea to fulfill all their duties well. They were always in places that they were needed. Often, by happenstance, they would be in the United States for meetings or trainings and would arrive just in time for a funeral or family gathering. The time seemed to work out for them.

They also had time to enjoy together. Hēhea, Tangiteina and 'Akesiu at the church sponsored celebration ball held in Salt Lake City, Utah.

They were an active part of the lives of their family and friends as well as in their calling in the church.

Tonga Toutai and Hēhea with Maka and Teiko Fonua. Teiko was Tonga Toutai's school mate when he moved to Nuku'alofa to go to school and had been instrumental in helping Tonga Toutai learn more about the gospel. They remained friends for the rest of their lives.

Lu'isa Hēhea Kona'ī first met Tonga Toutai and he proposed to her right after a dance. Their courtship was short but their marriage was founded on commitment, hard work and singleness to building the kingdom of God in Tonga. They worked side by side through every challenge. Tonga Toutai depended on her love and support as he accepted new responsibilities. Hēhea supported him so he could fulfill his responsibilities freely. Their marriage is one of the great love stories among the saints in Tonga.

Chapter 7

Endure to the End | 1990 - 2002

If thou wilt do good, yea, and hold out faithful to the end, thou shalt be saved in the kingdom of God, which is the greatest of all the gifts of God.
Doctrine and Covenants 6:13

Missionary Training Center

Missionary efforts continued to grow, and the Kingdom of Tonga still had a surplus of young people willing to serve missions. It was necessary to build a Missionary Training Center in Tonga to prepare future missionaries for the rigors of missionary work.

On January 15, 1990, Tonga Toutai was set apart as the President of the Tonga Missionary Training Center. The Missionary Training Center in Tonga was located near the Pāletu'a home. They could often hear the melodic singing of the missionaries during devotionals from their home.

Tonga Toutai and Hēhea provided training to future missionaries but were also open to instruction. In a letter from Elder Ben Banks to the Pāletu'a's, he praised them for their ability to accept feedback from him on ways to improve work at the training center. Tonga Toutai was always open to counsel from church leaders and accepted correction and feedback with grace. For him, doing what was right was always more important than being right.

The 100 year celebration of the Church in Tonga included special programs and this rare opportunity for former mission presidents and their wives to gather on Tongatapu. They are pictured here with visiting authority, Elder Russell M. Nelson. Left to right: Patrick Dalton, John H. Groberg, James Christensen, Tonga Toutai Pāletu'a, Elder Russell M. Nelson, Sione Latū, Pita Hopoate, Melvin Butler, Eric B. Shumway, 'Isileli Tupou Kongaika. Almost thirty years of missionary service is represented in this picture. (Kinikini Collection)

100 Years of the Church in Tonga

1991 was a year of celebration for Tongans all around the world. Various celebrations were being held for Tongan saints in Tonga, Australia, New Zealand, Hawaii, California, Utah, Texas, and wherever faithful Tongan saints lived. The celebrations were large and expansive.

Tonga Toutai had lived to see fifty years of church growth in the Kingdom of Tonga. From small branches to the building of Liahona College, the organization of the first stake, the expansion of missionary work to the building of a Temple. He had seen the transition from church meetings that were held in traditional Tongan huts into brick and mortar chapels. He saw travel change from canoes and boats to airplanes. Communication with church headquarters had changed from monthly letters by boat, to telephone calls, and in a few years correspondence through the internet. So many things had changed, and yet he remained mindful of those who had sacrificed so much to bring the gospel to Tonga.

During the centennial ceremonies in Tonga, he offered a "prayer of thanks" attended by church leaders and the royal family. His diary records the words from the prayer he offered on that occasion:

> Heavenly Father, we are grateful and humbled...for bringing the missionaries, all the mission presidents, who came and gave their lives.

Farewell Brother Ermel Morton

As time progressed, the friends from a lifetime of service began to pass away. During a visit to Salt Lake City in 1992, Tonga Toutai and Hēhea received word that their friend, Ermel Morton, had passed away. Brother Morton was the principal of Liahona when it opened and initiated the call for Tonga Toutai to leave his post with the Education Department of Tonga to teach at Liahona High School. A decision that completely changed their lives. Brother Morton was a dear friend and mentor.

Ermel Morton was a powerful instrument in helping the Tongan people. As a young man, he had served as a missionary in Tonga from 1936-1939. He returned to Tonga with his family to serve as a missionary and Principal of Liahona High School. He also translated the Book of Mormon, Doctrine and Covenants, and the Pearl of Great Price into the Tongan language.

The graveside services for Ermel Morton were held on March 27, 1992, in Mapleton, Utah. Tonga Toutai and Hēhea attended the service, and the Morton family asked if he would offer the prayer at the gravesite. The following was his prayer, as shared by Lorraine, Brother Morton's daughter.

> Our Father in Heaven, we are thy children. We gather together here beside this grave here to say farewell to our beloved brother Ermel Morton.
>
> We feel our gratitude, Father, for this great man. He was the one who came down and translated the Book of Mormon, Doctrine and Covenants, and Pearl of Great Price for the people of the islands of the sea.
>
> Father, we appreciate, very much, for your kindness to bring this man to Tonga, the island of the sea, and his family to sacrifice their lives to God their King.
>
> We are the lost sheep, but there was a plan to send some of the missionaries to come and get us. We are here today to say thanks for Ermel Morton for his sacrifice and his family, for the island of the sea, and all the people who helped him.
>
> Father bless us with humble hearts like this man so we

> can do better, so we can love one another, so we can try to improve the gospel in this life.
>
> Father, we love your Son, the sacrifice for, and because of us. We know this gospel is true. We're thankful for the prophet Joseph Smith who has sacrificed his life to build up your kingdom. We thank thee for a living prophet today, Ezra Taft Benson, and his two counselors and the Quorum of the Apostles and those that assist him and prepare for this conference next month. We thank thee Father for our precepts and the priesthood leaders. We are here together to say our appreciation and thanks for one of our brothers who leave us.
>
> Bless us with humble hearts so we can love one another, to build up our kingdom. This is the plan, and we ask thee in the name of thy Son Jesus Christ, our Redeemer. Amen.

It was a fitting tribute to a man who loved the Tongan people. Ermel Morton's efforts have brought light and knowledge to generations of Tongans. The timing of having Tonga Toutai and Hēhea's visit to Utah was a gift and a blessing.

Heavenly Father is in Charge

Tonga Toutai and Hēhea had lived a wonderful life. They had served in various callings and witnessed miracles occur along the way. The Lord was mindful of them and had blessed their family. Everything seemed to be going well as they were growing older, and seeing a younger generation of leaders take the reins of leadership.

But just as they experienced throughout their lives, things change. Death came to the Vainuku family on June 3, 1995. The young, handsome, athletic Nukuluve Pāletu'a Vainuku, one of Tonga Toutai and Hēhea's grandsons, suffered critical injuries from playing rugby. He was fourteen years old.

Nukuluve suffered pain for a while before he passed away. 'Akesiu shared the following about his passing:

> He (Nukuluve) returned home and said he felt pain in his body. So we took him to the hospital... the Dr. asked me to leave the room so he could talk to Mapa. As soon as Mapa came out of the room, I knew Nukuluve had passed away. But I believed Luve would still live.
>
> I called Tonga and Hēhea to come with some oil. When

Tonga Toutai, Nukuluve Pāletu'a Vainuku (child) and Hēhea in front of the temple. (Kinikini Collection)

they arrived, I watched on as Tonga Toutai held Luve close to his chest and told him, "Luve, come back! Come back, Luve!"

As I was watching, I knew that Luve could be healed. I had seen my father heal people. My father kept calling to him, but Luve's eyes remained closed.

My father then turned to me, and he said, "Siu, Luve is not coming back."

Then he said, "We can cry, and we can pray, but Heavenly Father is in charge."

I wanted to die. I wanted to die to let my son live. I felt my work was done. I wanted so badly for him to live, but I knew my father was right. The Lord is in charge.

Nukuluve passed away before the Sabbath.

Tonga said, "Nukuluve is honoring the Sabbath day, and we will do preparations for his burial on Monday." So we returned home (Vaisa "'Akesiu Interview").

Tonga Toutai's reference to Nukuluve passing away before the Sabbath is associated with the strict observance of the Sabbath day by Tongans.

Greeting old friend, President Gordon B. Hinckley at the Pioneers of the Pacific Celebration in 1998. (Kinikini Collection)

Preparations for Nukuluve's funeral and burial were planned, and a family-owned plot of land was chosen. Tonga Toutai named the plot of land, Nukuluve.

After a lifetime of witnessing the miraculous love and power of God, Tonga Toutai knew that it was Heavenly Father who was in charge.

Visits From Dear Friends

Tonga Toutai and Hēhea had a daily routine. They would wake up, prepare for the day, eat breakfast, pray, and serve in the temple. During this time, Tonga Toutai records he met Elder Oaks in the temple on November 18, 1996. In 1997 Tonga Touta records the following:

> November 13 - In the early evening there was a knock on the door, and it was Elder Packer (Boyd K. Packer). He had come to visit Tonga, and during the meeting he asked the people in the meeting where I was. So, he came to see me in my home. He came in, we talked and visited. He gave me and Hēhea a blessing. It was a blessing to see an Apostle of the Lord in my home (Paletu'a, diary).

Hēhea and Tonga Toutai during their final years. Picture taken in Hawaii during the Pioneers of the Pacific Celebration in 1998. (Kinikini Collection)

Elder Packer would visit again in 1995 and stop by the home to chat with Tonga Toutai and Hēhea. He would give them blessings at that time as well.

Pioneers of the Pacific Celebration BYU-Hawaii

In October 1998, a celebration was held on the campus of BYU-Hawaii, celebrating 150 years of the church in Polynesia. Tonga Toutai and Hēhea were invited as special guests. They were able to reconnect with friends they had made over a lifetime.

The celebration was also a conference that featured more than 200 presenters sharing information about the growth of the gospel in the islands. Among the presenters were, Chieko Okasaki, formerly a member of the general Relief Society presidency, Elder Adney Y. Komatsu, Elder Glen L. Rudd, and many others.

It was a wonderful opportunity to meet, reflect, and connect with friends from the past.

Review of the translation of the Book of Mormon

A review of the Book of Mormon in the Tongan language was needed. Tonga Toutai and Hēhea were asked to review the translation and make corrections as needed. This would be the first time a native speaker would review the translation and make corrections. He was contracted by the church to begin this work. In conjunction with other Tongan language translators in other parts of the world, they worked to clarify the scriptures for future generations of Tongans.

Final years

Tonga Toutai and Hēhea lived in their home close to the temple. He continued to work in the Temple every day that it was open. He also continued to provide Patriarchal blessings and temple Sealings.

> Tuesday, December 14, 1999 - We woke up, said prayers, ate breakfast, and then went to the temple to work. When we finished, we returned home and made some food. After that, I gave three patriarchal blessings. We then cleaned our home, ironed our clothing, and in the evening we attended a program hosted by the High Priest (Pāletu'a, diary).

Tonga Toutai and Hēhea kept a consistent schedule of working in the temple up until Tonga Toutai passed away.

On December 15, 2002, after dinner, Tonga Toutai told his sweet wife Hēhea he was going to rest. He passed away peacefully in his sleep.

He was buried in Nukuluve, near to his grandson on the family plot of land close to the temple.

His sweet wife Hēhea passed away a few years later, on May 16, 2005, in Laie, Hawaii. They are buried together.

Chapter 8

Epilogue

If thou wilt do good, yea, and hold out faithful to the end, thou shalt be saved in the kingdom of God, which is the greatest of all the gifts of God.

Doctrine and Covenants 6:13

Posterity

The legacy of Tonga Toutai and Hēhea continues in their children and posterity. Tonga Toutai and Hēhea only had two children: Tangiteina and 'Akesiu. Tangiteina and Pita had ten children, and 'Akesiu and Tēvita Mapa had twelve children. Those children have had children as well, and currently, as of 2019, there are over one hundred and ten great-grandchildren of Tonga Toutai and Hēhea Pāletu'a.

The grandchildren and some of the great-grandchildren have served missions in Tonga, New Zealand, Australia, Chile, Argentina, and throughout the United States.

As of this writing in the summer of 2019, twin great-grandsons of Tonga Toutai and Hēhea, (who were raised in Utah) received mission calls to serve in the Nuku'alofa Tonga Mission. This is in fulfillment of Tonga Toutai's desire for his posterity to return to Tonga to help strengthen the church in the islands.

Tongans Outside of Tonga

Like their Polynesian ancestors, Tongans eagerly travel and establish new roots in new lands. A large group of Tongans moved to Salt

Lake City, Utah, during the 1960s through the 1980s. These Tongans established themselves in communities. Soon Tongan wards were set up to meet the needs of Tongan saints. The first Tongan ward in Salt Lake City was called, Matavai'moui, in remembrance of the first branch in Tonga. As the Tongan population grew in Salt Lake City, more Tongan wards were formed. These wards belonged to *papālangi* stakes.

Soon there were enough Tongan wards in Utah to establish a Tongan stake. In 1993 President Thomas S. Monson and Elder John H. Groberg established the Salt Lake Utah Tongan Stake. It was a great blessing to the Tongans who had moved to Utah to be closer to the church. The first Stake President of the Salt Lake Utah Tongan Stake was Tonga Toutai and Hēhea's son-in-law, Pita Kinikini. President Groberg's counsel to Tonga Toutai in the 1960s while serving as a counselor in the mission presidency was fulfilled; everything turned out okay.

There was a clear connection between the new Tongan Stake in Salt Lake City, Utah, and the pioneering efforts from the saints in Tonga. The first stake in Tonga was organized in 1968 with Elder Groberg and President Monson. The new stake in 1993 was also established by these loving leaders. The meeting to organize the stake was also filled with memories by President Monson about establishing the first stake in Tonga. He also shared the need for Tongans to cling to the faith of their fathers. The new stake also covered three counties: Utah County, Salt Lake County, and Davis County. Similar to the three Tongan districts: Tongatapu, Ha'apai, Vava'u.

Much like the stakes in Tonga, the stake in Utah would also see a surge in membership activity and a need for expansion. In time the Salt Lake Utah Tongan Stake would be divided into two stakes; the north stake and the south stake. Eventually, it was divided again into three stakes. In 2019, another division was announced with the addition of a few more Tongan stakes. Currently, there are five operating Tongan Stakes in Utah.

The formation of Tongan stakes in Utah did not come without controversy. Questions often arise about why a Tongan Stake should exist at all if we are to be one people in the gospel. These conversations largely occur by people outside of Tongan Stakes. This question has existed since the organization of the first Tongan wards in the valley. Despite the controversy, the Lord has blessed Tongan saints in Salt Lake with places they can worship, maintain their cultural identity and honor their heritage. While these Tongan saints serve Tongans, the stakes welcome all people. A Samoan branch was included in the Tongan Stake in Utah County, and people from various backgrounds (Caucasian, Hispanic, African-American, Samoan, etc.) are members of these stakes.

The descendants of Tonga Toutai and Hēhea Pāletu'a after viewing the movie "The Other Side of Heaven 2: Fire of Faith" raising their hands and shouting, "Hurrah for Israel." 'Akesiu and Tangiteina are seated in the center surrounded by their children, grandchildren and great-grandchildren. (Kinikini Collection)

Other Side of Heaven 2: The Fire of Faith

Tonga Toutai's life was depicted in the movie, The Other Side of Heaven 2: The Fire of Faith. The movie captures the essence of Tonga Toutai's faith and conversion, although the movie was influenced by the artistic storytelling of the people who created the film.

The Pāletu'a family was consulted for information about Tonga Toutai and his life; however, they were not directly involved in the creation of the script or movie. Information and pictures were shared, and correspondence provided information on music, dancing, and the background of Tonga Toutai and his family.

The posterity of Tonga Toutai and Hēhea gathered for a special family screening of the film a few days before it was released to the general public. They were surprised to learn that Tonga Toutai's character was a main character in the film. They were informed by Elder Groberg that his story was in the movie earlier. However, they did not know to what extent. They were pleasantly surprised by the outcome. After the

Elder John H. Groberg introduced Tangiteina and 'Akesiu before the world-wide premier of the movie "The Other Side of Heaven 2: Fire of Faith" to a packed theater in Sandy, Utah. (Kinikini Collection)

Tēvita Mapa and 'Akesiu family with Tonga Toutai and Hēhea. (Kinikini Collection)

Pita and Tangiteina family. (Kinikini Collection)

movie, the posterity of Tonga Toutai and Hēhea posed for picture and video with a shout of, "Hurrah for Israel."

Two days later, Tangiteina and 'Akesiu were invited by Elder Groberg to attend the worldwide premiere in Sandy, Utah. Government dignitaries, church leaders, and others filled the theater to watch the movie together with the actors and the Groberg family. Elder Groberg lovingly recognized Tangiteina and 'Akesiu during the opening of the film.

The faith that Tonga Toutai and Hēhea instilled in their children and grandchildren were now being passed on to future generations.

How would Tonga Toutai feel about his portrayal in the film? According to Tangiteina and 'Akesiu, he would be very pleased. The message of the film centers on themes of family, fathers and sons, and, more importantly, Heavenly Father and Jesus Christ. These are the things that mattered most to him.

Missionary Work Continues

While the missionary work has been successful in the kingdom of Tonga, work remains to be done. Missionaries are still being called to serve. It is estimated that every home in Tonga has been visited by the missionaries at least once. Tonga has the highest percentage of members of the church per capita of any other nation in the world, and yet, missionary work continues.

Tangiteina returned to Tonga as a proselyting missionary in 2007. She visited Ha'afeva, Pangai, 'Uiha, and the small island of Mo'unga'one, the island of the Pāletu'a family. There she met an old woman who recognized her name. She asked Tangiteina if she was the daughter of Tonga Toutai Pāletu'a. She replied, "yes." The woman then said, "Why do you keep coming here to teach us? First, your father was here, then your daughter came, and now you have come?" Tangiteina replied, "Because this is true. And if you are not baptized after I go, my grandchildren will come, and their children will come until you are baptized. We come because this is true." The old woman scoffed, but Tangiteina invited her to be baptized and bore testimony that God loved her.

Tangiteina heard later that the old woman was baptized shortly after their visit. She passed away two weeks later.

Setting apart President Fatani and his wife Milika Mafi with Elder Gary E. Stevenson. Tangiteina and 'Akesiu attended. Milika is a Pāletu'a and is named after Tonga Toutai's mother. June 2019. (Kinikini Collection)

Tongan Mission Presidents

In June 2019, Tangiteina and 'Akesiu attended a meeting to set apart the mission president of the Papua New Guinea mission. They were invited by the wife of the new mission president. Elder Gary E. Stevenson of the Quorum of the Twelve Apostles laid his hands on President Fatani's head and then on his wife, Milika Mafi's head, to pronounce a blessing. She is a Pāletu'a. She is Tonga Toutai's niece. She is named after Tonga Toutai's mother. And she will now carry on a Pāletu'a family tradition of sharing God's word as a *faifekau*, to the people of Papua New Guinea.

Conclusion

Tonga Toutai and Hēhea's story is only one from several early Tongan saints. The gospel work in Tonga was (and remains) a collective effort. Throughout history, Tongan members of the church have been working together in a common cause. People with equally remarkable experiences surrounded Tonga Toutai, histories with the power to inspire, convert and heal.

Tongan pioneers like Misitana Vea, Sē Saulala, Sione Tu'ikolongahau, Siosifa Naeata, Siosaia Mataele, Kitione Maile, Filimone Tupou, Metuisela Tua'one, Sālesi Vānisi, Sione Tomasi, Paula Langi, Militoni Fonua, Tēvita Pauni, Tupou Kapetaua, and so many more. They have all carried the spirit of Tongan faith and testimony. Their stories need to be told. We are responsible to tell them.

There is a Tongan proverb, "*Mo'ui manatu ki ho tupuanga*," which means "to live remembering your roots." Looking at the past gives us depth and purpose in the tasks ahead. I urge all people, but specifically, those of Tongan heritage, to look back in order to move forward.

There are current generations of Tongans that may never visit the kingdom of Tonga or learn to speak the language. For those of us in this transitional phase of knowing our cultural heritage and living outside of the kingdom, we have the *fatongia* (responsibility) of bridging those worlds. We can make the stories of our ancestors understandable to future generations. Their stories are our stories as long as we tell them. My desire is that all Tongans will more fully understand the profound faith and testimony from the Pacific.

Pictures 1980 - 2002

Tonga Toutai and Hēhea served as Temple President and Matron from 1983 - 1987.

Hēhea was a devoted grandmother who loved her grandchildren and spent time caring for them.

The building of the Temple in Tonga was exciting for members of the church. They gladly volunteered their time willingly.

Following the example of the building missionaries from decades before, much of the work was performed by the members.

Tongans worked alongside contractors from the United States and from around the Pacific to build the Tonga Temple.

Pictures 1980 - 2002   131

Tonga Toutai represented the church in various functions around Tonga. Bearing testimony to the peole of Tonga in all occassions and also to the King of Tonga, King Taufa'ahau IV. In one instance, he broke the Tongan custom and did not place himself lower than the king (in height) to bear his testimony. It was not an act of defiance but an act of acknowledging that all men are subject to God.

The Temple provided more opportunities for Tongans to learn necessary leadership skills.

After the dedication ceremony the general authorities came out all dressed in whilte..

Watching on as the Angel Moroni is placed on top of the temple. It was a joyous occassion for the people watching. Spontaneous hymn singing occurred and the Tongan saints rejoiced.

Elder Gordon B. Hinckley arrived to dedicate the Tonga Temple as President Kimball was not healthy enough to make the trip.

Crowds of people were excited to attend the openhouse of the Temple.

A true friend, Tonga Toutai with the Elder John H. Groberg and his wife, Jean.

The dedication ceremonies were fulfillment of President David O. McKay's prophesy in 1955.

Pictures 1980 - 2002   135

Tonga Toutai and Hēhea loved spending time with their children and grandchildren. They loved the children. They also felt the most important thing they could do for them is to teach them the gospel at every opportunity.

Tonga Toutai with the grandchildren on the beach.

The Pāletu'a's traveled to Salt Lake City at least twice a year, sometimes more depending on their responsibilities. It was good time for them to visit with Tangiteina and the grandchildren.

Four generation picture. Tēvita Kona'ī, Hēhea, Tangiteina and Milika Mafi during her second birthday.

Pictures 1980 - 2002   **137**

Tonga Toutai and Hēhea dedicated their lives to serving the Lord in the kingdom of Tonga. Their work as missionaries began the day they were married as they were both set apart as missionaries at that time. They spent their entire lives continuing that missionary effort.

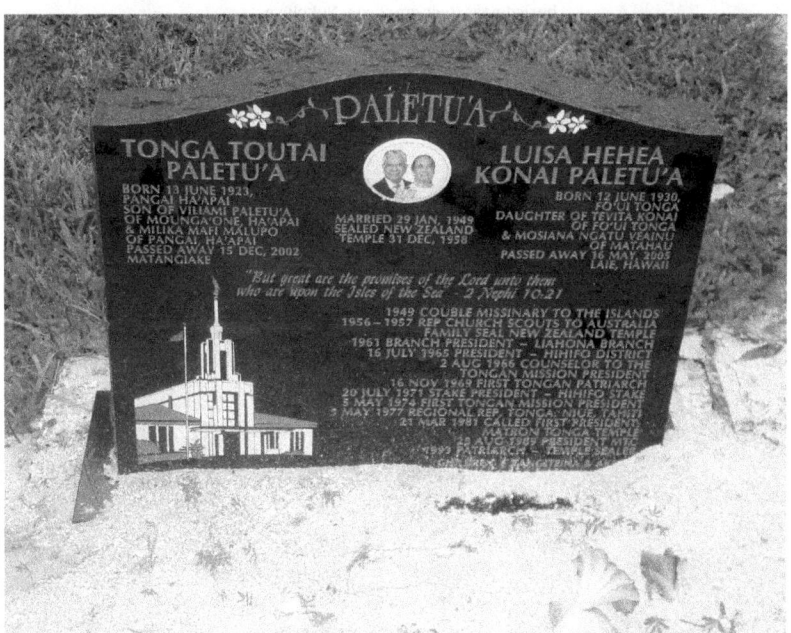

Tangiteina and 'Akesiu at the gravemarker for Tonga Toutai and Hēhea. They are buried near their grandson, Nukuluve.

Chapter Notes

Chapter 1 | Beginnings

1. The exact date of birth for Tonga Toutai has inconsistencies, even in his own personal records. In some of his documentation he lists his birthday as June 11 and other records it is listed as June 13. This was a common occurrence for Tongans born during the early 1900s. Births occurred at home. An official date of birth was recorded with the government; however, in remote areas, it would require travel to a capital city which was not always convenient. In some cases, children as old as four or five would be recorded in the government record with parents having to estimate the date of their actual birth. Determining this often meant recalling what was happening at that time of the child's birth (death of a family member, drought, hurricane, etc.) and then estimating a date. Genealogical records for Tongans during this time will often have inconsistencies. The author chose to use the date most often cited among Tonga Toutai's personal records.

2. The *mahaki faka'auha* (Spanish flu) was an epidemic that spread throughout the world. Globally it is estimated that it killed up to 100 million people. It arrived in Tonga on the SS Tulane. The following was recorded about the event, "The disease…brought Tonga to a standstill. Government and most businesses were closed, while plantations were overgrown with weeds as there were not enough able men to work. Church bells fell silent as no one was well enough to ring them. No wireless communications and the lack of newspapers meant no information about the illness, and potential treatments reached communities across the islands, and although the news was spread by word of mouth, the disease spread just as quickly." Queen Salote was in her first year of the reign when the Spanish flu arrived and in an interview with Elizabeth Bott Spillius she recorded the following, "There was no social life… people crept into their houses to die. Some died because they were too weak to get food. People were buried like dogs… no ceremonies, just bundled in graves. The people were distressed by having their dead buried in pits together that they were going around digging them back up again." The devastation was massive, killing roughly eight percent of the population in Tonga (Gee).

3. The absence of a mission president in Tonga resulted in near apostasy lead by three foreign and one native Tongan missionary. In addition to already suspicious views of the church in the Kingdom of Tonga from the monarchy, it would take years for the church (and members of the church) to be viewed in a positive light. Of the four missionaries that were disciplined (three foreign,

one Tongan) only information about the Tongan is available. He repented and returned to full fellowship. These events would have been widely known but would have been of particular interest (and gossip) to other congregations. The new mission president, Reuben Magnus Wiberg, had served as a missionary as a young man in Tonga from 1920-1925 during the time David O. McKay visited Tonga for the first time. Already familiar with the Tongan culture, President Wiberg immediately began working towards restoring the order in the church. Fortunately, with the previous limitations on foreign missionaries in the Kingdom of Tonga, many Tongan members were able to fill leadership positions.

4. Queen Sālote's refusal to meet with the Mormon missionaries appears customarily un-Tongan-like. The issues of the queen's legitimacy to the throne early during her reign were challenged by various parties, including the Parliament, the nobles and chiefs. Her request for the limitation of Mormon missionaries into Tonga was an outgrowth of an additional element of provocation for her reign. In Elizabeth Wood-Ellem's book on Queen Sālote she states, "Her request to Rodwell that no more Mormon missionaries be allowed to enter Tonga because they were a disturbing element in the kingdom was not clearly explained, but she may have suspected the American Mormons encouraged the 'democratic' tendencies of the 'Reactionary Party' (Wood-Ellem 91-91)." The uncertainty about Mormons and their supposed political agenda in Tonga would be a continuing issue beginning with the Passport Act which disallowed foreign Mormon missionaries from entering the country in the 1920s and again in the 1940s.

5. Historically, Tongans easily adopt foreign ideas into Tongan culture. When Wesleyan Tongans converted to mormonism, vestiges of their former religion would often influence their approach into the practices of their new faith. This is evident in the tradition known in the Church of Tonga as *Faka Mē*. The first Sunday of the month of May is set aside for the children to recite their memorized *lesonī* (lessons) to everyone in the congregation. The children wear white clothing for this special occassion. In the LDS tradition, the *Fake Mē* is replaced by the Primary program. LDS parents will also dress their children largely in white as well. No Primary Program in the LDS church has dress guidelines, but it is not uncommon to see this in Tongan wards or branches throughout the world. Noel Rutherford states the following in his book, *Friendly Islands: A History of Tonga*. "Political independence was coupled in Tonga with a large measure of cultural integrity. Of course, Tonga adopted 'ministers and nobles and parliaments' as well as 'apostles who live to sing and preach,' but these were absorbed with remarkably little dislocation into a way of life and a political system with its roots in remote antiquity. Tonga adopted many western ways, but somehow, they always seemed to finish up being more Tongan than western. To satisfy western notions, for instance,

Tonga had cabinet ministers, but their authority often came less from their new titles than from the fact that their ancestors in direct line had been exercising that sort of power for perhaps a thousand years. Similarly, Christian doctrines and denominational differences were tailored to meet Tongan needs, often to the despair of the missionary mentors (Rutherford ix-x)."

6. In May of 1935, three Elders from the United States arrived in Tonga to begin their mission service: Elders Thomas F. Whitley, Donald N. Anderson, and Floyd C. Fletcher. It was a much-needed enhancement for the work. These Elders were new, motivated, and came with special gifts to help the work progress. Elders Whitley and Anderson were assigned to work in Vava'u. Elder Floyd C. Fletcher remained in Tongatapu. Elder Fletcher was an avid scouter and was charged to organize the scouting program in Tonga. His efforts were modest but effective. Twenty years after he started scouting the Kingdom of Tonga would send a contingent of Tongan scouts to attend the worldwide Pan America Scouting Jubilee in Australia. This group would include Tonga Toutai Pāletu'a.

Chapter 2 | Conversion

1. The arrival of World War II in Tonga affected the Tongan people and culture in profound ways. Tongans were asked to move inland while soldiers and military personnel occupied the ports and the main cities. Members of the church were also given a curfew and restrictions on what they could do in the evening. The mission president's annual report states the following for 1941: "Since it has been forbidden to have lights at night, the missionaries have held cottage meetings in the afternoon and early evenings." The Western world was also introduced into Tongan culture. For the first time, Tongans were exposed to the concept of money, materialism and the concept of wealth. These concepts, previously foreign to Tongans, would be a concern for Queen Sālote and would be one of the motivating factors in her push for a return to cultural values and identity later in her reign.

2. Tonga Toutai's decision to return home to tell his parents about his desire to be baptized follows the Tongan attribute of *faka'apa'apa* (respect). To do something as drastic as joining another church without his parent's knowledge would be considered disgraceful and a sign that he was not raised correctly by his parents. It was out of respect for his parents and family that he returned home to tell them about his desire to be baptized. It is important that the reaction of Viliami and Milika toward Tonga Toutai's baptism is steeped in love, not anger. The motivations for their behavior are imbued in their cultural beliefs that value respect, love, loyalty, and family. In a culturally collective

society, every individual is a part of a whole system. Individual choices always consider how a choice affects others. Tonga Toutai's choice to be baptized disrupted the family and religious system for the Paletu'a family. To maintain order within Tongan society, everyone has a role to fill, and Tonga Toutai was stepping out of his role.

    3. Pīliote Kona'ī was serving a mission in Ha'apai beginning in 1945 as the Faleloa Branch President. His family visited him frequently to take supplies to him. In 1949 his sisters, Tangivale, Siale and Hēhea visited him. It is assumed that Tonga Toutai and Hēhea met during the area conference in April. It would have the most concentrated members of the church in one place at the same time. Pīliote was also one of the main speakers at the conference.

    4. Traditional Tongan marriages were often formal arrangements that required much time, effort, family involvement, and ceremony. For Tonga Toutai and Hēhea, their marriage agreement was simple and without fanfare. Hēhea came from a humble family, and Tonga was just beginning his career as a young educator. Traditionally marriages are sponsored by the groom's family, but Tonga Toutai did not have familial support. Tonga Toutai was also characteristically practical and would only do what needed to be done. The reaction from Hēhea's father to ask his daughter what she wanted to do seemed to indicate he had a profound trust in Hēhea's judgement, thus allowing her to marry someone she did not know very well.

    5. Makeke was initially established as a tool for missionary work in 1924. It was a successful endeavor prompting the building of a new and larger school, Liahona College. The original Makeke school was then transferred to the new property and turned into Liahona College. It would be called Liahona College until 1961 when the name would officially change to Liahona High School.

    6. The Book of Mormon translation into the Tongan language was performed and completed by 1939 lead by a young missionary named, Ermel Morton. He was assisted by church leaders in Tonga. He then took the manuscript to President George Albert Smith who approved of the translation. Tongans believed that the Tongan Book of Mormon would be available quickly; however, Prince Tupouto'a (later King Tuafa'ahau IV) returned from Australia and began to established a formalized way the Tongan language was written. For example, these changes included eliminating the "b" and replacing it with a "p." Earlier translated works were not changed. For example, the Holy Bible retained the "b" and is still printed as, *Tohi Tabu*, instead of *Tohi Tapu*. The printing of the Book of Mormon into the Tongan language was placed on hold until the prince made the official changes. The Book of Mormon was printed in April 1946 almost seven years after the translation was completed.

Chapter 3 | Forward with Faith

    1. Queen Salote's famous carriage ride after the coronation of Queen Elizabeth is probably the most recognizable act she is known for outside of Tonga however inside of Tonga, it is only a small portion of what she was able to accomplish. Queen Salote was younger than Queen Elizabeth at her own coronation. It is probable that Queen Salote recognized a future for the young queen similar to her own path. Of the event, Queen Salote recorded the following: After the coronation, we were led to an annexe of the Abbey (Westminster) and offered a light meal…It was now beginning to rain. When we had finished eatching the rain seemed heavier. By the time we reached the carriages, it was drizzling. After about 15 minutes, rain fell for perhaps 20 minutes. It drizzled one more; then there were bouts of heavy rain until the procession reached the Palace. The kind policemen who were looking after the procession asked the occupants of each carriage if they would like the hood of the carriage put up, and they all said they would. But when we were asked about our carriage – and fortunately I was the one who was asked – I was so caught up in the warmth of the people and the feelings of grace flooding my heart from the recent ceremony that I could not bear to be excluded from any part of that day, good or bad. Everything on that day was a treasure. I did not think to ask the chief (the Sultan of Kelantan), and he maintained silence with good grace. I apologized to him a few days later, and he accepted my apology gladly. That day we were both saturated with rain, but we were happy." The queen's company received flowers, cards, and jounalists who arrived around midnight inquiring of the queen's wellbeing. She was seated at a coronation dinner with Sir Winston Churchill and his wife later during the visit, and it was during this coronation dinner that Queen Salote had an opportunity to talk to Queen Elizabeth and invite her to Tonga. She accepted and visited the islands in December of that year. The impromptu actions by Queen Salote demonstrate the spirit of Tongans towards living in the moment, being aware of others, humility and love. It is no wonder Queen Sālote had the respect and love of her people and exemplified what it means to be a true Tongan (Wood-Ellem).

    2. Tonga Toutai and Hehea had two children, both daughters. Tangiteina and 'Akesiu. They would later *pusiaki* Tangiteina's second daughter, also named Hēhea.

    3. The building of Liahona was a mammoth undertaking both physically and financially. The scope of the project was enormous. Only government schools were financially supported. Religious schools existed but were usually underfunded and existed on a smaller scale. Liahona was a large school with multiple buildings that required skilled laborers from outside of Tonga to help build it. The Kingdom of Tonga was going through a cultural renaissance with an emphasis on maintaining Tongan culture and embracing education. The

Crown Prince Tupouto'a, the Minister for Education in Tonga, lead the charge by establishing various schools in the country. He desired to provide Tongans with as much education as possible. His encouragement for the building of Liahona, despite opposition from nobles, was a driving force in helping the school secure permissions necessary to build (Wood-Ellem 225).

4. Evon Huntsman's account of traveling to Tonga from the United States with Elder LeGrand Richards provides insight into the difficulty of reaching the islands.

5. The act of giving items (even if it does not belong to you) for free is not an uncommon trait for Tongans who place a high value on relationships. Material items are of little consequence in a collective society where everything is shared property. The act of the man telling Tonga Toutai to take the materials for free was a gesture of love and affection to him and in no way represents a tactic to defraud his employer. In a culture where sharing is more important than possessing, offering items is a demonstration of respect.

6. There is a discrepancy in Tonga Toutai's records about the date he attended the Scouting Jamboree in Melbourne, Australia. The date he gives in the book, Tongan Saints: A Legacy of Faith, states he attended the Jamboree in 1959. Mission records, journals, and third-party journal accounts indicate that the date of these events occurred in 1955. Further research discovered that the Pan Pacific World Scout Jamboree in 1959 was held in Auckland, New Zealand, and not Melbourne, Australia.

7. The New Zealand Temple was dedicated on April 20-22, 1958 by David O. McKay. Saints from the Pacific were encouraged to go to New Zealand to receive their Temple ordinances. While New Zealand was the closest temple, the trip was costly. Tongans worked hard and sacrificed much to attend the temple. Many of those accounts have been recorded in other sources. The Paletu'a family would be the second group of Tongan saints that would go to the temple. Fortunately, Tongans residing in Fiji and New Zealand helped to house, feed, and transport visiting saints to defray some of the cost.

Chapter 4 | Preparing the Way

1. Strict observances were held when Queen Salote passed away. Tongans, not only in Tonga but elsewhere mourned. The queen traveled to New Zealand on November 4, 1965, on an Argosy aircraft at the personal request of Queen Elizabeth II to seek medical care. Silent crowds gathered on both sides of the road from the Palace to Fua'motu airport, a 21-kilometer road, to say goodbye to the queen. She passed away in New Zealand. When her body was being returned back to Tonga for burial the Tongans who lived in New Zealand

honored her at the airport. It was reported, "black-clothed Tongans wrapped in large waist-mats seated on the rain-soaked tarmac, the sun bleaming fitfully in a leaden sky while the coffin was carried aboard (Wood-Ellem 291)." The kingdom mourned her death for months.

2. The Stake President of the first Tongan Stake in Salt Lake City, Utah, would be Pita Kinikini, Tonga Toutai's son-in-law. The words of President Groberg had been fulfilled. Tangiteina and Pita would be all right, and the Lord had a plan for them.

3. The parable of the *makafeke* was a favorite story from President Thomas S. Monson. He shared it often. The makafeke also comes from Tongan lore. The story is told that there was a very clever rat traveling in the ocean on a boat. While traveling, his boat began to sink. Being scared of the water, he noticed an octopus. He asked the octopus to take him to land by allowing him to ride on the octopus' head. The octopus agreed. When they arrived at the island, the rat refused to pay the octopus. The shape of a *makafeke* resembles the silhouette of a rat. This folktale explains why the *makafeke* works.

4. During Tonga Toutai's first visit to Salt Lake City for General Conference, he also met other church leaders and their wives. He has a picture with the wife of Joseph Fielding Smith in his records. He also received his Patriarchal Blessing through Eldred Smith in Salt Lake City.

Chapter 5 | Missionary Work

1. There are two references in this section of Tonga Toutai "laying it on the line" for his missionaries and an instance where he *tafulu'i* (to firmly correct someone) when the saints did not recognize the importance of an Apostle visiting Tonga. This is not uncommon behavior from those who know Tonga Toutai. He could be very forward, and curt towards those he believed should know or behave better. He could be unrelentingly demanding, not only of himself but of others and expected the very best one could offer. A story is told of a church meeting where someone in the congregation was being sustained to a leadership calling. Tonga Toutai did not believe that person should hold such a calling. During the sustaining, when asked if anyone opposed, he raised his hand and stood up to be acknowledged. Priesthood leadership stopped the meeting. They met with him privately, and the matter was resolved. Tonga Toutai was known to be very straight forward, and that was a characteristic that endeared him to Tongans. No one had to guess where they stood with him because he would happily tell you the truth.

2. The Area Conference was designed for the prophet and church leaders to preach the gospel to those who were unable to attend the General Conference

sessions in Salt Lake City. During the Area Conference, President Kimball urged saints to "make Zion bloom where you are." The indication was for Tongans to work toward spiritual self-sufficiency. In April of 1974, President Kimball revealed his desire for each nation and country to be self-governing and to extend work beyond their borders to other areas. The desire was for each nation to have enough missionaries to serve in their country and extras to be sent abroad. Historically, with the constant restraints from the government on the quota for foreign missionaries, The Kingdom of Tonga had already relied on their own people to run the affairs of the church. Tonga had already progressed toward that goal (Britsch 492).

    4. As of the writing of this book, in 2019, the missionaries that served during the *"Ta'u oe kau Leimana"* (Year of the Lamanite) hold an annual reunion to remember and reminisce about that time in their lives. They have been holding the reunion for almost three decades, which has increased in size and scope since. It is held every year, usually after the church's general conference in April. The reunion in 2019 was held in the San Francisco Bay area in April. Over 300 people attended the three-day event from all over the United States, Australia, and Tonga. Every day was filled with events from performances, traditional dances, eating, speeches, and firesides. Stories were shared. A memorial list of the missionaries who passed away was read during the fireside. This group of missionaries has been gathering together every year in various locations including; Salt Lake City, Hawaii, Texas and a plan to return to Tonga when the Tonga Neiafu Temple is dedicated.

Chapter 6 | The Tonga Temple

    1. During the construction of the temple in 1981, Hēhea became ill. Teina flew to Tonga with three of her children in December to spend time with her parents.

    2. Temple work for Tonga Toutai's parents and siblings occurred as soon as it was possible. Tonga Toutai performed these ordinances himself with his wife. It is important to note that information about ordinances for the Paletu'a family on Family Search are incorrect. For example, Viliama Paletu'a's baptismal and initiatory work is listed as being performed in 1995 and 1997. Tonga Toutai's journal indicates that he performed all of the ordinances for his father a year after Viliami's death in 1973 before and after the October General Conference in the Salt Lake City Temple. In addition to this, Milika Mafi, Tonga Toutai's mother, passed away on May 26, 1967. All the dates in her records on Family Search indicate she was baptized in 1949 (18 years before her death) and that she received her initiatory, endowment, and sealing to

parents in the 1950s in the Laie, Hawaii Temple. This information in Family Search is incorrect. The author notes the importance of documenting these errors in the Family Search records. Tonga Toutai was articulate about his record keeping, and so it is mentioned here to clarify that the records, as they currently appear in Family Search, are inaccurate.

    3. The information for 'Ulamoleka's baptism in family search is incorrect. He was baptized in Matangiake by Tonga Toutai, and there is a photo documenting his baptism date. Fortunately, we know the date of his (and his wife 'Ana's) baptism to be July 31, 1982.

Chapter 7 | Preparing the Way

    1. The 100-year celebration of the church in Tonga was a worldwide event for Tongans. Celebration ceremonies were held in Australia, New Zealand, Hawaii, California, Utah, and other places. The scope of the celebration was enormous, with dances and performances, orations, speeches, and feasting. The event in Salt Lake City held a fireside at the Salt Lake City Tabernacle on Temple Square. The event was attended by President Monson and Elder John H. Groberg. Video footage of the Salt Lake Celebration exists with various wards performing and the daily events held at the Utah State Fairgrounds to accommodate the size of the crowd.

    2. While Ermel Morton is known to Tongans as the man who translated the Book of Mormon into the Tongan language, it should also be noted that he devoted his life to service in many other areas. His obituary from March 23, 1992, reports the following: Received degrees from Brigham Young University (BA and MA), and Indiana University (Ph.D.) Worked as a news reporter at Salt Lake Telegram, 1942-44. Taught at BYU 1944-46; Ricks College, 1946 to retirement in 1980. Served as a missionary in the Tongan Mission 1936-39; missionary and principal of Liahona College, Tonga, 1951-57; member of the Tongan Board of Education 1952-1957; member of the Pacific Board of Education 1957-60; missionary, Seattle, Washington 1983-84. President of the Ricks College Missionary Training Center 1969-76. Served as a High Counselor, temple ordinance worker, and in the name extraction program. Translated the Book of Mormon, Doctrine, and Covenants, Pearl of Great Price, into Tongan. Served as Patriarch in the Rexburg East Stake and then the Ricks College Second Stake from 1980 until his death. Ermel Morton served the people in the Kingdom of Tonga in many ways and his contributions of service in the fields of education and with the translation of the scriptures in the Tongan language has blessed generations of Tongans past, present and future.

3. The cause of Nukuluve's death was not explored at the time; however, since he was speaking and interacting with family for a while before he died it is believed he suffered from internal injuries.

4. The Sabbath day is a day of rest in Tonga. The Kingdom of Tonga has a law that prohibits business transactions, working in the garden, dances and other activities on the Sabbath Day. Tongans use the day to attend church services, participate in devotionals or firesides, and visit families. No businesses are open on that day. One can usually tell what day it is in Tonga based on what is happening. For example, on Saturday, in preparation for Sunday, people often clean their homes and yards in preparation for the Sabbath day. They take the refuse and rubbish and burn it. The smell and sight of things burning from various homes is a good indication that people are preparing for the Sabbath Day.

5. The Pioneers of the Pacific celebration gathered saints from all across the pacific to La'ie, Hawaii on the campus of BYU-Hawaii.

6. An evaluation of the Tongan translation of the Book of Mormon was performed in 1995. Ermel Morton's work had withstood decades of missionary work. Tongans, in 1995, were asked to revisit the Book of Mormon, evaluate the language pertaining to the original language, and make recommendations. The work required Tongans that knew and understood both Tongan and English to make the comparisons. Tonga Toutai was selected to help in this process. In the end, Brother Morton's work remained largely unchanged during this process.

7. The author visited Tonga Toutai and Hēhea in the fall of 1999. A request was made at that time to Tonga Toutai to take his recorded material and preserve it. Tonga Toutai and the author spent a few hours going through pictures and the documentation discussing what they meant. Despite their age, Tonga Toutai and Hēhea were healthy. Upon arriving in Tonga, the author attended a wedding sealing ceremony that Tonga Toutai officiated in the Nuku'alofa, Tonga Temple.

Chapter 8 | Epilogue

1. The posterity of Tonga Toutai and Hēhea continue to contribute in various capacities to church service. Missionary service has been an essential part of the family tradition. Most of the grandchildren served missions to various parts of the world. Tangiteina, eldest daughter of Tonga Toutai began serving as a senior missionary after her husband passed away in 2000. She has served a total of eleven missions at the time of this book with plans to serve another mission to Tonga. Her missions have included serving various missions at the Family History Library in Salt Lake City, three missions to

Tonga (two temple missions and one prosyleting), a mission in Sāmoa (temple) and Nauvoo, Illinois. His posterity has also included church service as Stake President, Bishops, High Council, Relief Society Presidencies, Primary Presidencies, Scouting, Youth, etc.

    2. The migration of Tongans outside of Utah have created large populations of Tongans in New Zealand, Australia, California, Texas, and Utah. There are Tongans in other areas of the world as well, but most have relocated with other groups of Tongans. The Tongans that came to Utah were mainly members of the Church of Jesus Christ of Latter-day Saints; however, there is also a large population of Tongans in Utah that belong to the Methodist and Seventh-Day Adventist congregations.

    3. Controversy about having Tongan wards and stakes are common concerns that are discussed in Utah congregations by members, usually outside of the Tongan Stake. The author has heard these conversations advocating for a unified church that does not "segregate" Tongans members from local wards. The author chooses to view the issue as allowing Tongans to worship relative to the "dictates of their own conscious." This allows Tongans to worship and honor their heritage, supported by others of the same cultural heritage.

    4. The movie, The Other Side of Heaven:Fire of Faith, depicts the conversion story of Tonga Toutai; however, the family was not consulted for information about Tonga Toutai's history until after the movie was filmed. When consulted, the filmmakers did their best to make the adjustments, although some were too late to make. For example, in the movie, Tonga Toutai's father is named, Sione (John). In real life, his name was Viliami (William). When this was discovered, the filmmakers tried to see if they could make the change with the name in the movie, but it was too difficult to do. They did, however, include the name "Viliami" at the end of the film in print form when explaining what happened to him afterwards. Discrepancies in the film include the following: burying Tonga Toutai on the beach, the events of his baptism, as well as the timeline of events. Tonga Toutai was a father with two teenage daughters and had been a member of the church for over twenty years when he was called to serve as a counselor to John H. Groberg in the Mission Presidency in the 1960s. Despite these discrepancies, the spirit of the film was embraced by the descendants of Tonga Toutai and Hēhea Pāletu'a when they viewed the film as a family at a private screening.

The Priesthood Line of Authority

Tonga Toutai Pāletu'a was ordained a High Priest, September 6, 1968, by Thomas S. Monson.

Thomas S. Monson was ordained an Apostle, October 10, 1963, by Joseph Fielding Smith.

Joseph Fielding Smith was ordained an Apostle, April 7, 1910, by Joseph F. Smith.

Joseph F. Smith was ordained an Apostle, July 1, 1886, by Brigham Young.

Brigham Young was ordained an Apostle, February 14, 1835, under the hands of three witnesses, Oliver Cowdery, David Whitmer and Martin Harris, "who were blessed by the laying on of hands of the Presidency (Joseph Smith, Sidney Rigdon and Frederick G. Williams) to choose the Twelve Apostles"; D&C 18:37: History of the Church, Vol. 2 pp. 187-188, after which the Presidency laid their hands upon them and confirmed their blessings and ordinations. (Times and Seasons, Vol. 6 p. 868).

Joseph Smith and Oliver Cowdery received the Melchizedek Priesthood in 1829 from Peter, James and John.

Glossary of Tongan Words

A list of Tongan words and their definitions to help the reader understand certain terms.

faifekaku - a minister or preacher. Also means missionary.
faka'apa'apa - often translated into English as "respect." It is the respect a person of toward another person in the Tongan community.
fakatapu - usually the beginning of a speech, expressing the speakers respect to those present.
fatongia - responsibility and work for the benefit of someone of a higher social rank without reward or compensation.
fetokoni'aki - to help one another, to co-operate.
hokohoko – genealogy. Family history.
kāinga - originally used to describe a group of people united under the rule of one chief. Can also be used to describe people of a shared belief system. *Kāinga lotu* describes people of the same church.
kātoanga - festival, public festivity or celebration.
kavenga - a burden or a load. The responsibilities carried out to sustain and support another.
lahi - literally means "big" but can also be used at the end of a name to refer to 'senior.' *loufau* - ribbon. In this case, a ribbon used to tie a sister missionary's hair up.
mahaki faka'auha - refers to the Spanish flu that spread throughout the world and killed eight percent of the population of Tonga.
makafeke - an octupus catcher. Usually a shell wrapped with a stick and cord used to dangle over the side of a boat. The octopus, mistaking it for food will wrap its tentacles around it and the fisherman can pull it up and place it in the boat with little difficulty.
mamonga - the tongan version of the word "Mormon."
mana - power, spiritual power, authority. Supernatural qualities of authority and divinity.
nofo ā - a term used at a farewell the person leaving speaks to a person is his remaining behind.
pangai - originally "center" or "root." Later used to describe meeting places. Also a location. The home of the Pāletu'a family.
papālangi - persons of European descent; white person. Foreigner.
pusiaki – often refers to a person who has been informally adopted and raised by someone other than their parents. A common practice among Tongans is to allow another family member to raise a child either because one is unable to have children, their parents have passed away or because the family member asks.
si'i - literally means "small" but can also be used at the end of a name to refer to 'junior.' Many children who carry the same name of an older person will have

the term "si'i" added to the end of their name as a way to differentiate them from the senior.

si'i kai ha - Tongan proverb meaning that it is better to appear with something small than to wish for something extravagent and not show up at all.

takipō -wake, all-night watch, on the occasion of a royal death. The palace is surrounded by men holding lighted torches.

tafulu'i - to reprimand. Usually in a harsh and aggressive way.

tupenu - a cloth worn around the waist.

ta'ovala - piece of matting worn around the waist over the *tupenu*. Formal attire for Tongans.

References

'Alatini-Richter, Faahi Kihelotu. "Second Annual Conference Mormon History in the Pacific." Mormon Pacific Historical Society, *Mormon History in the Pacific: Proceedings ..*, 1981, pp. 57–59, scholarsarchive.byu.edu/cgi/viewcontent.cgi?referer=https://www.google.com/&httpsredir=1&article=1028&context=mphs.

Britsch, R. Lanier. Unto the Islands of the Sea: A History of the Latter-Day Saints in the Pacific. Deseret Book, 1986.

Collocott, E. E. V. "Marriage in Tonga." *The Journal of the Polynesian Society*, vol. 32, no. 4(128), 1923, pp. 221–228. *JSTOR*, www.jstor.org/stable/20701939.

Campbell, I. C. Island Kingdom: Tonga Ancient and Modern. Canterbury University Press, 1992.

Gee, Eleanor. *Three months of horror: a century since the Spanish flu ravaged Tonga.* MatangiTonga. 4 Dec. 2018. https://matangitonga.to/2018/12/04/three-months-horror-century-spanish-flu-ravaged-tonga

Goodman, Michael A. "Church Growth in Tonga: Historical and Cultural Connections." *Regional Studies in Latter-Day Saint Church History: The Pacific Isles*, Brigham Young University, 2008, pp. 37–54.

Groberg, John H. *Anytime, Anywhere.* Deseret Book, 2006

Groberg, John H. *Eternity is Now.* Covenant Communications Inc., 2016.

Groberg, John H. *The Fire of Faith.* Bookcraft, 1996.

Huntsman, Evon. *My Story Lest I Forget.* Huntsman-Gifford.com. 2002. http://www.huntsman-gifford.com/history/evonw/evonw.htm

Kinikini, Siope L. "Lu'isa Hehea Paletu'a Interview." 5 Jan. 2005. (Video available)

Kinikini, Siope L. "Teina Interview." 24 Jun. 2019.

Kinikini, Siope L. "Groberg Interview." 23 April 2007.

Koloi, Malakai. *Remembering school days, courting in Tongan islands.* News Mail Australia. 16 February 2018. https://www.news-mail.com.au/news/remembering-school-days-courting-in-tongan-islands/3337526/

"Manatumelie mei Pakineti Ngatuvai." Created by Pakineti Ngatuvai. Facebook, Uploaded by Pakineti Ngatuvai in the Tau' Oe Kau Leimana Facebook group page. 1 June 2019. https://www.facebook.com/groups/652427188262394/

Mapa, Tēvita Uatahausi. "Tongan Oral History Project." Ha'apai, Pangai, 11 Jan. 1974.

Morton, Helen. "Having Children." *Becoming Tongan: An Ethnography of Childhood*, University of Hawaii Press, 1996, pp. 64–65.

Nixon, Shirley. *Diary (The Nixons in Tonga, Liahona High School, January 1962-July 1968).* Author's personal collection

Paletu'a, Tonga Toutai. "I Couldn't Hold Back the Tears." *The Ensign Magazine,* Dec. 1975.

Pāletu'a, Tonga Toutai, *Diary of Tonga Toutai Pāletu'a, 1950-2000.* Author's personal collection

Rutherford, Noel. "Friendly Islands: A History of Tonga." *Friendly Islands: A History of Tonga*, Oxford University Press, 1977, pp. ix-x.

"Seminar for Temple Presidents Gives Instruction, Inspiration." *LDS Church News*, Sept. 1982, www.churchofjesuschrist.org/study/ensign/1982/11/news-of-the-church/seminar-for-temple-presidents-gives-instruction-inspiration?lang=eng.

Shumway, Eric B. *Tongan Saints: Legacy of Faith.* Institute for Polynesian Studies, 1998.

S.L. Utah Tongan Stake Organization. 1993. Video. Authors personal collection.

Tonga Nuku'alofa Mission manuscript history and historical reports, 1891-1976; Volume 1, 1891-1955; Part 1, 1891-1897, 1920-1936; Church History Library, https://catalog.lds.org/assets?id=e958e-ac4-9200-4545-8f4e-63bfd18ea43d&crate=0&index=0 (accessed: April 18, 2019)

Tonga Nuku'alofa Mission manuscript history and historical reports, 1891-1976; Volume 1, 1891-1955; Part 2, 1937-1949; Church History Library, https://catalog.lds.org/assets?id=f5340d33-055d-4d82-a128-84cc928fa081&crate=0&index=0 (accessed: April 18, 2019)

Tonga Nuku'alofa Mission manuscript history and historical reports, 1891-1976; Volume 1, 1891-1955; Part 3, 1949-1955; Church History Library, https://catalog.lds.org/assets?id=073b-25de-f00b-4afe-b9d2-fbe8b0c41669&crate=0&index=0 (accessed: May 10, 2019)

Tonga Nuku'alofa Mission manuscript history and historical reports, 1891-1976; Volume 3, 1964-1976; Part 2, 1971-1976; Church History Library, https://catalog.lds.org/assets?id=a0e60b8b-1841-4def-bf13-6b6dd501dcc8&crate=0&index=0 (accessed: June 19, 2019)

Vaisa, Vika F. "'Akesiu Vainuku Interview." 15 May 2019.

Wood-Ellem, Elizabeth. Queen Sālote of Tonga: The Story of an Era 1900-1965. Aukland University Press, 1999.

Whitley, Colleen. *Thomas Farrar Whitley's Mission Photos of Tonga, 1935-1938*, vol. 48, no. 1, 2009, pp. 89–121., doi:https://byustudies.byu.edu/content/thomas-farrar-whitleys-mission-photos-tonga-1935-1938.

www.ingramcontent.com/pod-product-compliance
Lightning Source LLC
Chambersburg PA
CBHW060642150426
42811CB00078B/2246/J